SOUPS
FOR EVERY SEASON

SOUPS
FOR EVERY SEASON
Recipes for your hob, microwave or slow-cooker

ANNETTE YATES

ROBINSON

ROBINSON

Originally published in the UK in 2003 as *Super Soups and Sauces* by Right Way,
an imprint of Constable & Robinson

This edition published in Great Britain in 2014 by Robinson

A CIP catalogue record for this book is available from the British Library.

ISBN 978-1-71602-386-9 (paperback)
ISBN 978-1-71602-387-6 (ebook)

Typeset in Great Britain by Mousemat Design Limited
Printed and bound by CPI Group (UK) Ltd, Croydon, CR0 4YY

Robinson
is an imprint of
Constable & Robinson Ltd
100 Victoria Embankment
London EC4Y 0DY

An Hachette UK Company
www.hachette.co.uk

www.constablerobinson.com

Contents

Contents

Introduction

A bowl of soup makes a delicious dish at any time of year. In winter it can be comforting and substantial, in summer it can be light and refreshing. Soup is so easy to cook and to eat and is a wonderful way to make the most of seasonal produce. Buying foods grown in our own country – preferably locally sourced when possible – not only means they taste at their best but also that they are better value and help to reduce the cost of transporting produce halfway round the world – both from a financial and an ecological point of view. Some hearty soups make a complete meal, perhaps served with some crusty bread, others can form a light lunch, followed by some bread and cheese, a sandwich or a crisp salad, and others can make a perfect starter to awaken your tastebuds before the main course of a special meal.

Soups for Every Season is a collection of tempting recipes created to use the best seasonal produce available because while some foods are produced all year round, many of them have times of year when they are at their best and most flavoursome. There are many classics – ones that everyone should have in their repertoire – and others that are more innovative, using unusual blends of flavours and textures to create mouthwatering bowlfuls that will surprise and tantalize. Whether you have a glut of beans or tomatoes in the garden, like to pick your own produce at a local farm, or buy from your local supermarket, farm shop, or farmers' market, making soup is always a great way to enjoy plenty of vegetables (and sometimes fruit) as well as sustainably sourced fish (which is also a seasonal product) and meats.

The lovely thing about soups is that nothing is etched in stone. You can vary ingredients according to what you have to hand or what you grow yourselves. Be creative – we have been – and you'll be thrilled with the results you achieve.

1 Notes about the Recipes

- For best results, use one set of measurements – metric or imperial.

- All spoon measurements are level, unless otherwise stated.

- All vegetables and fruit are medium-sized unless otherwise stated.

- Always wash, trim, peel, core and deseed, as necessary, fresh produce before use.

- Eggs are medium-sized unless otherwise stated.

- When potatoes are called for, use a good all-round, fairly floury variety such as Maris Piper, unless otherwise specified.

A word about stock:
In the recipes, where two types of stock are listed – for instance, I may suggest using chicken stock or vegetable stock – these are the ones I have tested, with my preference listed first. However, you will want to use the stock of your own choice (if you are a vegetarian, for example, you will not want to use chicken stock). The result may be different but it will be just as delicious. Or you may want to use a gluten-free or other free-from stock cube.

Hot stock:
Use hot stock, unless it is an uncooked soup (so if you make up a stock cube, granules or concentrate, dissolve it in boiling water from a kettle, then add it to the other ingredients). This is not vital when cooking conventionally, though it shortens the cooking time, but is particularly important when microwaving or slow-cooking.

Puréeing soups:

When puréeing soup in a food processor or blender, you will probably need to do it in batches.

Adjusting the consistency of soups:

The consistency of the finished soup can vary slightly. Since ingredients, saucepans, hobs and microwaves vary, it is always a good idea to have some extra stock or liquid handy, so that you can thin the soup to the desired consistency, if necessary.

Microwave instructions:

When a recipe is appropriate, and most are, microwave methods have been given. Make sure you use a microwave-safe casserole dish.

The recipes have been tested in a microwave oven with a wattage of 700–800W. If your microwave has a lower wattage, you will need to cook for a little longer. If it has a higher wattage, then simply lower the power level slightly and cook for the time given in the recipe. All cooking is on High unless otherwise stated. Medium-High is equivalent to 500–600W, Medium is 350–400W and Medium-Low is 200–300W.

Always use microwave-safe containers, such as pyrex, or oven-to-table porcelain. Avoid ironstone (it will absorb microwaves), dishes with gilt or silver edging or metal containers.

Freezing:

Freezing instructions are given for all suitable recipes. Always cool the soup quickly – you can stand the pan in a shallow bowl of cold water to speed the process, if you like – and freeze as soon as possible in freezerproof containers with sealable lids, and labelled clearly. Once thawed and reheated, adjust the seasoning to taste.

2 Making your own Stock

Stock is the basis of most soups and many savoury sauces. Making your own stock can be a rewarding pastime and there is no doubt that a good home-made stock produces a soup or a sauce with a unique flavour. So when time allows, or when you have the ingredients to hand, it's worth making up a large quantity. The portion that you don't use can be reduced by gentle boiling, then cooled and frozen in small blocks for a later date within three months.

Cartons of fresh stock are available in the chilled cabinets of large supermarkets. Some of them are very good and they contain little salt, sugar or artificial additives.

What about stock cubes, granules and concentrates? Most of us are very busy people and, although we may make stock from time to time, we often resort to using 'instant' stock. Liquid concentrates may be a better option than cubes or granules as they tend to be richer in flavour but lower in salt. However, the choice is yours. Just remember that it would be a shame to ruin your wonderful soup by adding a cheap stock cube that may add little more than salt and colouring. Choose one with a good balance of flavours that is not too high in salt and, if you are using this type of stock, always taste your soup before adding any more salt – it is unlikely to need it.

Vegetable Stock

This recipe makes a light and delicate stock. Vegetables to use include onions, leeks, garlic, carrots, celery, celeriac, parsnips, cabbage, tomatoes and red or yellow peppers – whatever is in season. Vegetable trimmings can be used too (including mushroom stalks, celery tops, onion skins (if you are making brown stock), outer cabbage leaves and tomato skins) as well as fresh herbs.

Makes about 1 litre/1¾ pints

about 680g/1½lb vegetables, washed, peel left on and roughly chopped
10 black peppercorns
1 small lemon, roughly chopped
1 bouquet garni (see Cooks' tip on page 7)
salt and freshly ground black pepper

1. Put all the ingredients into a large saucepan, cover with 1.2 litres/2 pints cold water and season lightly with salt. Bring to the boil, skimming off any scum that rises to the surface using a large spoon. Partially cover, reduce the heat and simmer gently for about 45 minutes, occasionally removing any scum.

2. Use a very fine sieve or wet a piece of muslin, then wring out any excess water and use it to line a colander. Strain the stock through the sieve or colander.

3. If you plan to use the stock as it is, check the seasoning, adding salt and pepper to taste. If you plan to reduce the stock to give it a more concentrated flavour, tip it into a saucepan and bring to the boil. Simmer gently, skimming the surface as necessary, until the stock has reduced by about half. Adjust the seasoning as required.

4. Use at once, or cool quickly and chill for up to 3 days.

To microwave:
1. Put all the ingredients into a large casserole, cover with
1.2 litres/2 pints cold water and season lightly with salt.

2. Cover and cook on High for about 10 minutes or until the
mixture comes to the boil, stirring occasionally, then cook on
Medium-Low for 25–30 minutes.

3. As step 3.

4. If you plan to use the stock as it is, check the seasoning,
adding salt and pepper to taste. If you plan to reduce the stock
(for a more concentrated flavour), return it to the casserole and
cook, uncovered, on High for about 15 minutes or until the stock
has reduced by about half. Adjust the seasoning if necessary.

5. Use at once, or cool quickly and chill for up to 3 days.

To slow-cook:
1. Put all the ingredients into a slow-cooker, cover with
1 litre/1¾ pints boiling water and season lightly with salt.

2. Cover and cook on High for 2 hours or Low for 4 hours.

3. As steps 3–4.

To freeze:
Freeze the chilled stock in suitable quantities for up to 3 months.

Meat Stock

You can use raw or cooked bones for your stock. If you use raw bones, ask your butcher to chop them into small pieces. To give your stock extra flavour and richness, put the bones in a roasting tin with the onion – in its skin for extra colour – and carrot and roast in a preheated oven at 200°C/Gas 6 for about 30 minutes until browned before putting them in the saucepan with the remaining ingredients to makc the stock.

Makes about 1 litre/1¾ pints

about 1kg/2½lb raw bones, ham, pork, beef or lamb
1 onion, thickly sliced
1 carrot, thickly sliced
1 celery stick, thickly sliced or a few celery seeds
1 bouquet garni (see Cooks' tip on page 7)
10 black peppercorns
½ tsp salt

1. Put all the ingredients into a large pan and cover with about 1.7 litres/3 pints water. Bring to the boil, skimming off any scum that rises to the surface using a large spoon.

2. Partially cover, reduce the heat and simmer gently for about 2 hours, occasionally removing any scum.

3. Use a very fine sieve or wet a piece of muslin, then wring out any excess water and use it to line a colander. Strain the stock through the sieve or colander.

4. If you plan to use the stock as it is, check the seasoning, adding salt and pepper to taste. If you plan to reduce the stock (for a more concentrated flavour), tip it into a saucepan and bring to the boil. Simmer gently, skimming the surface as necessary, until the stock has reduced by about half. Adjust the seasoning as required.

5. Spoon off any fat from the surface, then cool and chill for up to 3 days.

To microwave:

1. Put all the ingredients into a large casserole, cover with 1.2 litres/2 pints cold water and season lightly with salt.

2. Cover and cook on High for about 10 minutes or until the mixture comes to the boil, stirring occasionally, then cook on Medium-Low for about 1 hour, occasionally removing any scum.

3. As step 3.

4. If you plan to use the stock as it is, check the seasoning, adding salt and pepper to taste. If you plan to reduce the stock (for a more concentrated flavour), return it to the casserole and cook, uncovered, on High for about 15 minutes or until the stock has reduced by about half. Adjust the seasoning if necessary.

5. As step 5.

To slow-cook:

1. Put all the ingredients into the slow-cooker, cover with 1 litre/1¾ pints boiling water and season lightly with salt.

2. Cover and cook on High for 3–4 hours or Low for 6–8 hours.

3. As steps 3–5.

To freeze:

Freeze the chilled stock in suitable quantities for up to 3 months.

COOKS' TIP: Bouquet garni

For convenience, you can buy sachets of dried bouquet garni, but why not make a fresh one? Simply tie together one or two bay leaves with some sprigs of parsley and thyme, rosemary or sage with kitchen string. Make sure you use less of strongly flavoured herbs, such as rosemary and sage, otherwise they will dominate.

Poultry or Game Stock

Raw bones are best for this stock but cooked carcasses produce good stock too. Making stock is a good way to get the most out of the Christmas turkey. For a golden colour, leave the skin on the onion. When making game stock, adding a pinch of cracked allspice or juniper berries gives an extra dimension to the flavour.

Makes about 1 litre/1¾ pints

1 raw or cooked chicken carcass, broken into pieces
1 onion, sliced
1 carrot, sliced
1 celery stick, sliced (when in season) or a few celery seeds,
a few sprigs of herbs, such as tarragon and thyme
2 bay leaves
2cm/¾in piece of fresh root ginger, peel left on and roughly chopped

1. Put all the ingredients into a large saucepan and cover with about 1.7 litres/3 pints cold water. Bring to the boil, skimming off any scum that rises to the surface using a large spoon.

2. Partially cover, reduce the heat and simmer gently for about 2 hours, occasionally removing any scum.

3. Use a very fine sieve or wet a piece of muslin, then wring out any excess water and use it to line a colander. Strain the stock through the sieve or colander.

4. If you plan to use the stock as it is, check the seasoning, adding salt and pepper to taste. If you plan to reduce the stock (for a more concentrated flavour), tip it into a saucepan and bring to the boil. Simmer gently, skimming the surface as necessary, until the stock has reduced by about half. Adjust the seasoning as required.

5. Spoon off any fat from the surface, then cool and chill for up to 3 days.

To microwave:
1. Put all the ingredients into a large casserole, cover with
1.2 litres/2 pints cold water and season lightly with salt.

2. Cover and cook on High for about 10 minutes or until the mixture
comes to the boil, stirring occasionally, then cook on Medium-Low
for about 45 minutes, occasionally removing any scum.

3. As step 3.

4. If you plan to use the stock as it is, check the seasoning, adding
salt and pepper to taste. If you plan to reduce the stock (for a more
concentrated flavour), return it to the casserole and cook,
uncovered, on High for about 15 minutes or until the stock has
reduced by about half. Adjust the seasoning if necessary.

5. As step 5.

To slow-cook:
1. Put all the ingredients into the slow-cooker, cover with
1 litre/1¾ pints boiling water and season lightly with salt.

2. Cover and cook on High for 2–3 hours or Low for 5–7 hours.

3. As steps 3–5.

To freeze:
Freeze the chilled stock in suitable quantities for up to 3 months.

COOKS' TIP: Pressure cooking
*A pressure cooker can reduce the cooking time of stock by about
half. Follow the manufacturer's instructions.*

Fish Stock

Home-made fish stock has a wonderfully delicate flavour. The best
fish for stock-making is white fish such as plaice, cod, haddock,
hake, sole, turbot and whiting. For a slightly smoky flavour, add a
small piece of smoked haddock or cod. For a good colour, leave the
skin on the onion.

Makes about 1 litre/1¾ pints

about 1kg/2¼lb fish bones, heads and trimmings
300ml/½ pint white wine
1 onion, sliced
1 carrot, sliced
1 small lemon, roughly chopped
2–3 parsley sprigs
2–3 fennel sprigs
2 bay leaves
10 black peppercorns
2 tsp caster sugar

1. Put all the ingredients into a large saucepan with 1 litre/1¾ pints
cold water. Bring to the boil, skimming off any scum that rises to
the surface using a large spoon.

2. Partially cover, reduce the heat and simmer gently for about
20 minutes, occasionally removing any scum.

3. Use a very fine sieve or wet a piece of muslin, then wring out any
excess water and use it to line a colander. Strain the stock through
the sieve or colander.

4. If you plan to use the stock as it is, check the seasoning, adding
salt and pepper to taste. If you plan to reduce the stock (for a more
concentrated flavour), tip it into a saucepan and bring to the boil.
Simmer gently, skimming the surface as necessary, until the stock
has reduced by about half. Adjust the seasoning as required.

5. Use at once or cool and chill for up to 2 days.

To microwave:
1. Put all the ingredients into a large casserole, cover with 600ml/1 pint cold water and season lightly with salt.

2. Cover and cook on High for about 10 minutes or until the mixture comes to the boil, then cook on Medium-Low for 10–15 minutes. Remove any scum.

3. As step 3.

4. If you plan to use the stock as it is, check the seasoning, adding salt and pepper to taste. If you plan to reduce the stock (for a more concentrated flavour), return it to the casserole and cook, uncovered, on High for about 10 minutes or until the stock has reduced by about half. Adjust the seasoning if necessary.

5. As step 5.

To slow-cook:
1. Put all the ingredients into the slow-cooker, cover with 1 litre/1¾ pints boiling water and season lightly with salt.

2. Cover and cook on High for 1 hour or Low for 4 hours.

3. As steps 3–5

To freeze:
Freeze the chilled stock in suitable quantities for up to 3 months.

3 Garnishes and Accompaniments

Hot or chilled, a soup can be transformed by a simple garnish. Though a garnish is essentially a decoration (adding colour, contrast and shape) it can also add texture, flavour, body and interest to a soup. In other words, it livens things up! Simply ladle the soup into serving bowls and add the garnish. Alternatively, serve one or more garnishes in separate bowls and pass them round the table for your guests to help themselves.

Garnishes:
Here are some ideas for attractive and tasty garnishes to get you started.

- Fresh herbs: Small sprigs, leaves or chopped. Choose herbs that will complement the soup. Try parsley, mint, chives, coriander, basil, tarragon, chervil or dill, or a mixture.

- Crisp-fried herbs: Sage leaves and parsley sprigs are best, washed, dried and lightly fried in oil for a few seconds until bright green and just crisp.

- Fresh edible flowers: Herb flowers in particular look pretty and taste good.

- Vegetables: Raw or blanched, they add colour and crunch. Try raw cucumber slices, chopped tomato (skinned and deseeded, see page 69), or small sprigs of watercress. Or what about blanched carrot strips, fresh peas or asparagus?

- Crisp-fried vegetables: Add extra flavour as well as colour and texture. Try thin onion rings; whole baby mushrooms; strips of leek, parsnip, or carrot; or wafer-thin slices (crisps) of potato, sweet potato or beetroot.

- Lemon, orange or lime slices: Shreds of citrus zest look and taste good too. Pour boiling water over them and leave to stand while you make the soup. Drain thoroughly, then scatter a few shreds on top of each serving.

- Cream, yogurt, fromage frais or crème fraîche: Swirl a spoonful on top of the soup. A sprinkling of chopped fresh herbs looks good over it too.

- Cheese: Freshly grated or shaved Parmesan and Cheddar are probably the best, but do try others (grated, crumbled or cut into tiny cubes) that complement the ingredients of the soup.

- Crispy bacon or pancetta: Small pieces of bacon, fried or grilled until crisp and crumbly. Remember that bacon is usually quite salty, so you are unlikely to need extra seasoning in the soup.

- Croûtons: See how to make them on page 16.

- Rice, pasta and other grains: Adding these makes a soup into a more substantial snack or meal, and it's a good way of using leftovers. Just before serving the soup, add some cooked rice or pasta shapes – add them hot to each serving bowl, or stir into the main body of the soup and heat through before serving. Cooked grains, like couscous and bulgar wheat, are ideal for using this way too.

- Nuts and seeds: Almond flakes, hazelnuts, pistachios and pine nuts are all delicious, fried or toasted. Try toasted seeds, like sesame, sunflower, pumpkin, caraway or fennel.

- Toasted coconut: This is good served with spicy soups. Lightly toasted shavings work better than desiccated coconut.

Breads:

The ideal accompaniment to soup is often a hunk of good, fresh (preferably warm) crusty bread. Bakers and supermarkets sell a huge range. For a change, why not choose from these? Or make your own to complement the flavour of the soup.

- Soda bread: Easy and quick to make.

- Traditional bread: Crusty or soft, white or wholemeal.

- Crusty baguette: Classic French loaves are good with or without garlic butter.

- Flavoured breads: Why not try cheese, tomato or olive bread?

- Italian-style breads made with olive oil: Ciabatta or focaccia are readily available in the supermarket.

- Pizza bread: Either make your own or buy a ready-made pizza base, brush it with plain, garlic or herb butter and grill until crisp and golden.

- Italian bread sticks: Buy them plain or flavoured.

- Bruschetta: Recipe on page 19.

- Indian breads: Plain or filled naan or chapattis, grilled or baked in the oven, are great with robust or spicy soups.

- Muffins: Serve them split and toasted.

- Hot garlic bread: Try the recipe on page 18.

- Hot herb bread: Make the recipe on page 18 with your favourite herbs.

- Melba toast: Ideal for serving with a light soup at the start of an elegant meal, see page 19.

Other accompaniments:
Don't be restricted by thinking you can only serve bread – be imaginative with your accompaniments.

- Samosas: Filled with spicy vegetables or a meat mixture and cooked until crisp.

- Filo parcels: Filled with cheese (feta or ricotta is good) and chopped fresh herbs, then fried or oven-cooked until crisp and golden.

- Chinese spring rolls: Crisply fried vegetable and beanshoot spring rolls.

- Croûtons: Make plain or garlic croûtons (see page 16).

- Cheesy toasts or croûte: Like mega-croûtons, these are small pieces of thickly sliced fresh bread, topped with grated cheese and grilled (try Parmesan, Cheddar or Gruyère)(see page 17).

- Potato pancakes: Grated potatoes mixed with flour, egg and milk and fried.
- Freshly baked scones: Plain, herb or cheese.

- Cheese sticks: Try our recipe on page 20.

- Dumplings: See Cock-a-Leekie with Mini Dumplings on page 130.

Croûtons

Use stale, firm-textured bread to make croûtons.

about 1 slice of bread per person
a little sunflower or olive oil

To fry:

1. Remove the crusts and cut the bread into small cubes.

2. In a pan, heat some sunflower or olive oil until hot, add the bread and cook, stirring gently, until crisp and golden brown. Drain on kitchen paper.

3. Once cooked and cooled, these croûtons can be kept in a sealed container for up to one week.

To toast:

1. Remove the crusts from the bread slices.

2. Toast the bread on both sides, then cut into cubes. Serve immediately.

To microwave:

1. Thinly spread both sides of two bread slices with butter (or brush lightly with olive oil) and remove the crusts. Cut the bread into 1cm/½in cubes.

2. Spread the cubes in an even layer on a heatproof plate. Cook, uncovered, on Medium-High for about 2–3 minutes, stirring once or twice until they just start to brown. The croûtons will continue to crisp up on cooling. These are best used on the day they are made or they will become hard.

> **COOKS' TIP: Garlic croûtons**
>
> *If you are frying croûtons, add some slices of garlic to the cooking fat as it heats up, lifting it out when it begins to turn brown. When toasting, try rubbing the bread with a split garlic clove before putting it under the grill. Alternatively, add some finely chopped or crushed garlic to the butter or oil before spreading it on the bread.*
>
> **COOKS' TIP: Parmesan croûtons**
>
> *Sprinkle some freshly grated Parmesan cheese over the freshly cooked, still-hot croûtons.*

Croûtes

Croûtes are like large croûtons – crisp and crunchy so ideal for serving with soup.

Serves 4

1 small baguette
50g/1¾oz butter, melted

1. Preheat the oven to 180°C/Gas 4.

2. Cut the baguette into 1cm/½in slices. Lightly brush both sides of each slice with melted butter and arrange them on a baking sheet.

3. Cook in the oven for about 10 minutes, turning them over once, or until crisp and golden brown.

Hot Garlic Bread

This method uses a French stick, but I have made garlic bread from all shapes and types of loaves.

Serves 8–10

1 large French stick
115g/4oz butter, softened
4 large garlic cloves, crushed or finely chopped

1. Preheat the oven to 200°C/Gas 6.

2. Make diagonal cuts into the bread, about 2.5cm/1in apart, without quite slicing it right through.

3. Mix together the butter and garlic and spread the mixture between the slices and, lastly, over the top of the loaf.

4. Wrap loosely in foil and cook in the oven for about 10 minutes until crisp and golden on the outside and soft in the centre.

COOKS' TIP: Hot herb bread
Follow the recipe for Hot Garlic Bread, omitting the garlic and adding 2–4 tbsp chopped fresh herbs – try parsley, thyme, chives, coriander, or a mixture. If you like, add a little finely grated lemon zest too.

Goats' Cheese Crostini

These are particularly good served with vegetable soups.

1. Toast thick slices of French bread on one side.

2. On the untoasted side, put a slice of chèvre or other goats' cheese and grill until bubbling. Serve immediately.

Melba Toast

Use stale bread for best results. Once cooled, Melba Toast can be stored in an airtight container for several days. Serve it with or without butter.

1. Using a grill or toaster, toast some bread slices on both sides until golden brown.

2. Cut off the crusts then, holding the toast flat, cut it horizontally into two thin slices. Cut each slice into 4 triangles.

3. Arrange the pieces, toasted-side down, on a grill pan. Toast until the edges curl and the toast is golden brown.

4. Serve warm or leave to cool on a rack.

Bruschetta

Use extra virgin olive oil for the best flavour.

Serves 6

6 large slices of country-style bread, such as ciabatta
1 large garlic clove
olive oil

1. Toast the bread until both sides are crisp and quite hard.

2. Halve the garlic clove and rub the cut sides over the bread so that the juice of the garlic is absorbed into the bread. Drizzle one side of each bread slice generously with olive oil.

3. Leave to stand for 5 minutes, then serve.

Cheese Sticks

Stored in an airtight container, these can be kept for up to one week.

Makes about 20

375g/13oz ready-rolled puff pastry, thawed if frozen
1 small egg, beaten
85g/3oz Parmesan cheese, freshly grated

1. Preheat the oven to 180°C/Gas 4.

2. Unroll the pastry and, using a sharp knife, trim off all the edges. Brush the pastry with beaten egg and sprinkle the cheese evenly over the top. Halve the pastry lengthways, then cut crossways to make about 20 strips.

3. Arrange the strips on a non-stick baking sheet, separating them slightly. Cook in the oven for about 15 minutes, or until puffed, misshapen and golden brown.

4. Cool on a wire rack.

Parmesan Crisps

Delicious little piles of cheese melted into crisp wafers.

Serves 6

115g/4oz Parmesan cheese, freshly grated

1. Preheat the oven to 200°C/Gas 6 and lay a sheet of baking paper on a dampened baking sheet.

2. Make 2 piles of the cheese, placed well apart, on the prepared baking sheet. Flatten each pile slightly, then cook in the oven for 10 minutes until melted. Remove from the oven and leave to cool and crisp.

3. Use the same day or store in an airtight container in the fridge.

4 Spring Soups

Many of the winter roots and greens are still available when the weather begins to get warmer, but it is also the time for the beginnings of the fresh spring crops. The first early carrots, spring greens, the first, tender nettles, sorrel and, of course, it's the season for majestic, sumptuous asparagus. Cauliflowers, although available throughout the year, are particularly good in spring and other crops, like purple sprouting broccoli, are at their best, too. Shellfish, such as clams, have been in season through the winter but brown crab come into their own, too, from spring through summer.

Vichyssoise

A delicious chilled soup made using delicate spring leeks. To achieve the traditional pale colour of Vichyssoise, only the white parts of the leeks are used – so when you are buying them, choose young specimens with large areas of white. If you are happy with a subtle pale green soup – and who wouldn't be when the flavour is so good? – you can use the trimmed green part as well.

Serves 6

25g/1oz butter
450g/1lb leeks, white part only, thinly sliced
1 onion, chopped
350g/12oz potatoes, peeled and thinly sliced
750ml/1¼ pints Chicken Stock (see page 8) or Vegetable Stock (see page 4)
salt and freshly ground black pepper
300ml/½ pint milk
150ml/1¼ pint single cream
snipped fresh chives, to garnish

1. Melt the butter in a large saucepan, add the leeks and onion and cook gently for 8–10 minutes, stirring occasionally, until soft but not brown.

2. Add the potatoes and stock and season with salt and pepper. Bring to the boil, cover, reduce the heat and simmer gently for 20–30 minutes until the vegetables are very soft, stirring once or twice.

3. Remove from the heat and stir in the milk.

4. Tip into a food processor or blender and purée until smooth. For a really smooth result, use a wooden spoon to rub the soup through a fine sieve. Leave to cool completely.

5. Stir in the cream, then chill the soup for at least 2 hours.

6. Serve garnished with chives.

To microwave:
1. Put the butter, leeks and onion into a large casserole, cover and cook on High for 5 minutes, stirring once, until soft.

2. Add the potatoes and half the hot stock and season with salt and pepper. Cover and cook on High for about 15 minutes, stirring occasionally, until the vegetables are very soft.

3. Stir in the remaining hot stock and then the milk.

4. As steps 4–6.

To slow-cook:
1. As step 1, then tip the leeks and onions into the crockpot.

2. Add the potatoes and hot stock and season with salt and pepper. Cover and cook on High for 2–3 hours or Low for 5–7 hours.

3. As steps 3–6.

Not suitable for freezing.

Asparagus Soup with Egg

Even during the short spring asparagus season, not every
bunch you buy will be at its absolute peak. If you find you
have some asparagus that is older and rather woody, this is
the perfect way to use it. You can serve the soup on its own,
but it does go particularly well with eggs.

Serves 4

450g/1lb asparagus
50g/1¾oz butter
1 large onion, finely chopped
about 750ml/1¼ pints Vegetable Stock (see page 4)
salt and freshly ground black pepper
150ml/¼ pint Greek-style plain yogurt
4 small eggs, hard-boiled

1. Cut the tips off the asparagus. Cook them in a little gently
simmering water for about 3 minutes, or until only just tender. Drain,
reserving the cooking water, then cool, cover and chill until needed.

2. Meanwhile, chop the asparagus stalks. Melt the butter in a large
saucepan, then add the asparagus stalks and onion. Cook gently for
about 5 minutes, stirring occasionally, until soft but not brown.

3. Make up the asparagus cooking water to 1 litre/1¾ pints with
stock. Add this stock to the pan and season with salt and pepper.
Bring to the boil, then cover, reduce the heat and simmer gently for
about 30 minutes until the asparagus is very soft.

4. Leave to cool slightly, then tip into a food processor or blender
and purée until smooth. Use a wooden spoon to rub the mixture
through a fine sieve to remove any stringy bits. Leave to cool.

5. Stir in the yogurt and adjust the seasoning to taste. Chill until
required.

6. Peel and quarter the eggs. Place four quarters in the bottom of each serving bowl, ladle the soup over them and top with the reserved asparagus tips.

To microwave:

1. Cut the tips off the asparagus. Put them into a small casserole with 2 tbsp water. Cover and cook on High for 2–3 minutes, or until only just tender, stirring gently once. Drain, cool, cover and chill until needed.

2. Meanwhile, chop the asparagus stalks. Put the butter, asparagus stalks and onion into a large casserole. Cover and cook for about 5 minutes, stirring once, until soft.

3. Add half the hot stock, then season with salt and pepper. Cover and cook on High for about 15 minutes or until the asparagus is very soft, stirring once or twice.

4. Add the remaining stock and continue as steps 4–6.

To slow-cook:

1. As steps 1 and 2, then tip into the crockpot.

2. At step 3, make the stock as before and make sure it's very hot. Pour over the vegetables. Cover and cook on High for 2 hours or Low for 4–6 hours.

3. As steps 4–6.

To freeze:

Cool after step 4, then freeze. To serve, thaw, stir in the yogurt and serve as step 6.

COOKS' TIP: Asparagus and ham soup

To make asparagus and ham soup, omit the eggs and replace the Vegetable Stock (see page 4) with a light ham stock. Place some slivers of smoked ham in the bottom of each bowl before adding the soup.

Sorrel and Spinach Soup

Sorrel is an often-forgotten vegetable that can be found from spring right through to early autumn. It can be cooked like spinach, made into a sauce or torn and tossed into salads. The leaves have a lovely, fresh, lemony flavour. It is easily grown in the garden. You could use lettuce instead of spinach in this delicately flavoured soup.

Serves 4–6

25g/1oz butter
1 onion, finely chopped
1 potato, peeled and thinly sliced
900ml/1½ pints Vegetable Stock (see page 4) or Chicken Stock (see page 8)
salt and freshly ground black pepper
175g/6oz sorrel leaves, coarsely shredded
175g/6oz spinach leaves, coarsely shredded
2 tbsp double cream, plus extra for garnish

1. Melt the butter in a large saucepan, then add the onion and cook gently for about 5 minutes, stirring occasionally, until soft but not brown.

2. Add the potato and stock, and season with salt and pepper. Bring to the boil, cover, reduce the heat and simmer gently for about 15 minutes, or until the potato is tender,

3. Stir in the sorrel and spinach and simmer gently for about 5 minutes until soft and wilted

4. Leave to cool slightly, then tip into a food processor or blender and purée until smooth. Adjust the seasoning to taste.

5. Return the soup to the pan, reheat and stir in the cream.

6. Serve with a small swirl of extra cream in each bowl.

To microwave:
1. Put the butter and onion into a large casserole, cover and cook on High for about 3 minutes, or until soft.

2. Add the potato and half the hot stock, then season with salt and pepper. Cook on High for about 10 minutes, stirring once or twice, or until the potato is very soft.

3. Stir in the sorrel and spinach, cover and cook on High for 3 minutes, stirring once.

4. Add the remaining stock and continue as steps 4–6.

To slow-cook:
1. As steps 1 and 2, then tip into the crockpot.

2. At step 3, make up the stock as before and make sure it's very hot. Pour over the vegetables. Cover and cook on High for 2 hours or Low for 4–6 hours.

3. Continue as steps 4–6.

To freeze:
Cool and freeze at the end of step 4. To serve, thaw, then continue as steps 5 and 6.

Nettle Soup

Use gloves when collecting nettles and pick the young tips only.
They are best in spring before they become too established and
tough. The soup is equally delicious hot or cold.

Serves 4

15g/½oz butter
1 onion, chopped
1 large potato, peeled and diced
1 colander full of nettle tips, about 25g/1oz, well rinsed
1 litre/1¾ pints Chicken Stock (see page 8) or Vegetable Stock (see page 4)
1 tbsp fresh thyme leaves
1 bay leaf
salt and freshly ground black pepper
a little freshly grated nutmeg
6 tbsp single cream
a little milk (optional)

1. Melt the butter in a large saucepan and fry the onion and potato
gently for 2 minutes, stirring, until softened but not browned.

2. Add the nettles, stock, herbs, a little salt and lots of black pepper.
Bring to the boil, reduce the heat, partially cover and simmer gently
for 15 minutes until everything is really tender.

3. Discard the bay leaf, then purée the mixture in a blender or food
processor. Return the soup to the pan and stir in the nutmeg and
4 tablespoons of the cream. Thin with a little milk, if necessary, and
season to taste with salt and pepper.

4. If you are serving the soup hot, return it to the saucepan and
heat through gently but do not boil. To serve it cold, chill it in the
fridge. Serve ladled into soup bowls with a swirl of the remaining
cream added to each bowl.

To microwave:
1. Put the butter, onion and potato into a large casserole, cover and cook on High for about 5 minutes until softening, stirring once or twice.

2. Stir in the nettles and cook on High for a further 2 minutes until slightly wilted. Heat the stock, then add half to the casserole with the herbs and season with salt and pepper. Cover and cook on High for about 10 minutes or until the potato is very soft, stirring once or twice.

3. Add the remaining hot stock, then continue as steps 3 and 4.

To slow-cook:
1. As step 1.

2. Tip into the slow-cooker and add the nettles, hot stock, herbs, salt and pepper.

3. Cover and cook on High for 1–2 hours or Low for 4–6 hours.

4. As steps 3 and 4. To serve, tip back in the slow-cooker and leave on Low until ready to serve.

To freeze:
Cool and freeze at the end of step 3. To serve, thaw completely, then continue as step 4.

Roasted Carrot and Chickpea Soup with Crumbled Feta

The young, early season carrots (bunched finger ones or Chantenay) have a lovely sweet flavour, which can be accentuated by roasting them instead of just boiling in the stock. You can simply boil them whole and use the stock to make the soup if you prefer. Rose harissa paste is flavoured with smoked paprika and rose water but the more fiery plain harissa paste can be used instead.

Serves 4

400g/14oz early baby carrots, trimmed and washed
2 tbsp olive oil, plus extra for drizzling
1 garlic clove, crushed
2 tbsp fresh thyme leaves
400g/14oz can chickpeas, drained
1 litre/1¾ pints Chicken Stock (see page 8) or Vegetable Stock (see page 4)
1–2 tbsp rose harissa paste
salt and freshly ground black pepper
115g/4oz feta cheese, crumbled
a few sprigs of fresh flat-leaf parsley, torn
lime wedges, for garnishing

1. Preheat the oven to 190°C/Gas 5.

2. Put the carrots in a roasting tin and toss in the oil and garlic. Sprinkle with the thyme, cover with foil and roast in the oven for 45 minutes until tender.

3. Tip the carrots into a large saucepan and add the chickpeas. Coarsely crush with a potato masher. Alternatively tip into a food processor and roughly crush them, then tip them into the pan. Do not purée – the texture should be rough.

4. Add the stock and harissa and simmer for 10 minutes.

5. Season to taste with salt and pepper. Ladle into soup bowls and top with the crumbled feta and the torn parsley. Serve garnished with lime wedges.

To microwave:
1. As step 2.

2. Tip the carrots into a large casserole and continue as step 3.

3. Add the hot stock and harissa, cover and cook on High for 5–10 minutes until boiling and full of flavour, stirring once or twice.

4. As step 5.

To slow-cook:
1. As step 2.

2. Tip the carrots into the slow-cooker. Add the hot stock and harissa. Cover and cook on High for 1–2 hours or Low for 4–6 hours.

3. Season to taste with salt and pepper. Ladle into bowls and top with the crumbled feta and torn parsley. Serve garnished with lime wedges.

To freeze:
Cool and freeze at the end of step 4. To serve, thaw completely, then reheat and garnish as step 5.

Cauliflower Cheese Soup

Cauliflowers are grown most of the year but are particularly good in spring. Use a well-flavoured Cheddar to give the soup a good, rich flavour. You could also try this recipe with broccoli, in season through the summer and autumn.

Serves 4

25g/1oz butter
1 onion, chopped
1 large potato, peeled and diced
1 small cauliflower, white part only, separated into small florets
750ml/1¼ pints Vegetable Stock (see page 4) or Chicken Stock (see page 8)
½ tsp made English mustard
4 tbsp dried skimmed milk powder
100g/3½oz strong Cheddar cheese, grated
salt and freshly ground black pepper
chopped fresh parsley, to garnish

To serve:
Croûtons (see page 16)

1. Melt the butter in a large saucepan. Add the onion and fry gently, stirring, for 3 minutes until softened but not browned.

2. Add the potato and the cauliflower florets and stock. Bring to the boil, reduce the heat, partially cover and simmer gently for 15 minutes, or until the florets are really soft.

3. Purée in a blender or food processor with the mustard, milk powder and cheese. Return to the pan and heat through gently, stirring.

4. Season to taste with salt and pepper. Ladle into warm bowls and garnish with a little chopped parsley. Serve with croûtons to sprinkle over.

To microwave:
1. Put the butter and onion in a large casserole and cook on High for 3 minutes, stirring once.

2. Add the potato, cauliflower florets and hot stock. Cover and cook on High for 10 minutes, or until the cauliflower is really tender, stirring once or twice.

3. As step 3. Return to the microwave to reheat for 1 minute.

4. As step 4.

To slow-cook:
1. As step 1.

2. Tip into the slow-cooker, add the potato, cauliflower florets and hot stock. Cover and cook on High for 2 hours or Low for 4–6 hours.

3. As step 3. Tip back in the slow-cooker and leave on Low for at least 5 minutes to heat through.

4. As step 4.

To freeze:
Cool and freeze at the end of step 3. To serve, thaw completely, then reheat thoroughly and garnish and serve as step 4.

Spring Vegetable Soup with Pesto Drizzle

As spring turns to summer, substitute red pepper for the swede and you could try some outer leaves of lettuce, shredded, instead of pak choi and a handful of baby broad beans or peas. This is definitely a soup that can be mixed and matched according to what's available.

Serves 4

175ml/6fl oz dry white wine
900ml/1½ pints Vegetable Stock (see page 4)
1 bunch of spring onions, chopped
2 early carrots, finely diced
½ small swede, finely diced
1 potato, finely diced
1 turnip, finely diced
1 large bay leaf
2 star anise
salt and freshly ground black pepper
2 heads of pak choi, finely shredded
2 tbsp green basil pesto
4–5 tbsp olive oil

1. Put the white wine in a large saucepan and bring to the boil. Boil rapidly for 2–3 minutes until reduced by half.

2. Add the remaining ingredients, except the pak choi, basil pesto and olive oil. Bring to the boil, reduce the heat, cover and simmer gently for 20 minutes until the vegetables are meltingly tender and the stock is well flavoured.

3. Discard the bay leaf and star anise. Add the pak choi and simmer for 2 minutes. Season to taste with salt and pepper.

4. Meanwhile, blend the pesto with the olive oil to form a pouring consistency, adding a little more oil if necessary.

5. Ladle the soup into warm bowls. Drizzle the pesto mixture on top of each one and serve straight away.

To microwave:
1. As step 1.

2. Tip into a large casserole, add half the hot stock and the remaining ingredients except the pak choi, basil pesto and olive oil. Cover and cook on High for 15 minutes, or until the vegetables are tender, stirring occasionally. Discard the bay leaf and star anise.

3. Add the remaining hot stock, cover and cook on High for 5 minutes, stirring once. Add the pak choi, cover and cook on High for a further 1 minute. Season to taste with salt and pepper.

4. Continue as steps 4 and 5.

To slow-cook:
1. As step 1. Tip into the slow-cooker.

2. Continue as step 2 but add hot stock. Cover and cook on High for 2–3 hours or Low for 5–7 hours.

3. Continue as step 3 but cover and leave on Low for 5 minutes to soften the pak choi.

4. Continue as steps 4–5.

To freeze:
Cool, discard the bay leaf and star anise, and freeze at the end of step 2. To serve, thaw completely, then bring to the boil, add the pak choi and continue as steps 3–5.

Kale, Radish and Haricot Bean Soup

The new season's radishes have a lovely, almost turnip-like flavour and are delicious cooked with kale in this hearty soup. Serve with crusty bread.

Serves 4

2 tbsp olive oil

1 bunch of spring onions, chopped

2 garlic cloves, chopped

1 tsp ground turmeric

1 tsp ground cumin

¼ tsp ground cloves

1 litre/1¾ pints Vegetable Stock (see page 4) or Chicken Stock (see page 8)

400g/14oz can haricot beans, drained

12 radishes, topped, tailed and sliced

1 bay leaf

salt and freshly ground black pepper

100g/3½oz kale, finely shredded, discarding the thick stumps

2 tbsp chopped fresh parsley

2 tbsp chopped fresh coriander

2 tbsp tahini paste

2 tbsp cornflour

2 tbsp water

150ml/¼ pint thick plain yogurt

a squeeze of lemon juice

1. Heat the oil in a large saucepan. Add the spring onions and fry, stirring, for 1 minute. Add the garlic and spices and fry for 30 seconds.

2. Stir in the stock, beans and radishes. Add the bay leaf, a little salt and plenty of black pepper. Bring to the boil, reduce the heat, partially cover and simmer gently for 15 minutes.

3. Add the greens, stir, and bring back to the boil. Reduce the heat, cover and simmer for a further 10 minutes until everything is really tender, stirring gently every now and then.

4. Discard the bay leaf. Stir in the fresh herbs and tahini paste until the paste melts. Blend the cornflour with the water and stir in. Bring to the boil and boil for 1 minute, stirring.

5. Add all but 4 tsp of the yogurt, reserving the rest for garnish. Spike with a squeeze of lemon juice.

6. Ladle into warm bowls and top each one with a small spoonful of the remaining yogurt.

To microwave:
1. Put the oil, spring onions, garlic and spices in a large casserole and cook on High for 1 minute. Stir.

2. Stir in the hot stock, the beans and radishes. Cover and cook on High for about 5 minutes until the soup comes to the boil, stirring once.

3. Season, add the kale and bay leaf, stir, cover and cook on High for 8–10 minutes until really tender, stirring occasionally.

4. Continue as step 4 but cook on High for 1–2 minutes, stirring once, to thicken. Continue as steps 5 and 6.

To slow-cook:
1. As step 1. Tip into the slow-cooker.

2. Continue as step 2 but season, add hot stock, beans, radishes, kale and bay leaf. Cover and cook on High for 2–3 hours or Low for 5–7 hours.

3. Continue as step 4. Tip back in the slow-cooker and cook on High for 15 minutes to thicken. Stir well.

4. As steps 5 and 6.

To freeze:
Discard the bay leaf and stir in the herbs and tahini at step 4. Do not thicken. Cool then freeze. To serve, thaw, reheat then continue as steps 4–6. Check seasoning, then serve.

Japanese-style Udon Noodle, Greens and Salmon

Spring greens are in high season. You can substitute pak choi or other shredded greens instead if you prefer. Pak choi will only need simmering for 2 minutes before adding the crab sticks. Look out for Surimi – Japanese crab sticks – in larger super-markets. They are made from sustainably sourced fish and have a good texture and flavour.

Serves 4

200g/7oz dried udon noodles
250g/9oz piece thick salmon fillet (sustainably sourced), skinned and cut in quarters
a little sesame oil
1.2 litres/2 pints Vegetable Stock (see page 4)
2 tbsp tamari or light soy sauce
2 tsp light soft brown sugar
3 tbsp mirin or dry sherry
1 tsp grated fresh root ginger
1 garlic clove, crushed
4 spring onions, chopped
1 head of spring greens, about 200g/7oz, trimmed and shredded
8 Surimi crab sticks or 4 ordinary ones, halved lengthways
1 tbsp miso paste
2 tsp toasted sesame seeds
a few coriander leaves, torn, to garnish

To serve:
sweet chilli sauce

1. Cook the noodles according to the packet directions. Drain and set aside.

2. Preheat the grill. Brush the salmon with the oil and cook under the grill for 3–4 minutes until just cooked through. Do not turn over. Set aside and keep warm.

3. While the salmon cooks, put all the remaining ingredients except the crabsticks, miso paste, sesame seeds and coriander in a large saucepan. Bring to the boil, then reduce the heat and simmer for 4 minutes. Add the crab sticks.

4. Blend a ladleful of the hot soup stock with the miso paste until smooth. Pour it back into the pan and stir gently. Taste and add more tamari, if necessary.

5. Pile the noodles in large soup bowls. Ladle in the soup, dividing the crab sticks and salmon evenly among the bowls. Sprinkle with sesame seeds and add a few torn coriander leaves. Serve drizzled with sweet chilli sauce.

To microwave:
1. As steps 1 and 2.

2. While the salmon cooks, put the remaining ingredients except the crabsticks, miso paste and sesame seeds, including hot stock, in a large casserole. Cover and cook on High for about 5 minutes until boiling, stirring once. Add the crab sticks.

3. As steps 4 and 5.

Not suitable for slow-cooking.

Not suitable for freezing.

French-style Fish Soup

Choose your favourite types of sustainably caught fish from the fishmonger or supermarket, making sure you select whatever is in season to get the best flavour. For this recipe, I've used sea bream or red mullet and prawns, all in season in spring. Ask the fishmonger to fillet the fish and keep the bones to make your fish stock (see page 10). You can, of course, use thawed frozen varieties if you prefer. Serve the soup immediately it has cooked, ladled on to the thick slices of toasted French bread.

Serves 4

25g/1oz butter
1 large onion, finely chopped
2 large garlic cloves, finely chopped or crushed
1 carrot, finely chopped
1 leek, thinly sliced
400g/14oz can chopped tomatoes
450ml/¾ pint Fish Stock (see page 10)
1 tsp dried mixed herbs
1 sea bream or red mullet, about 500g/1lb 2oz, filleted, skinned
and cut into bite-size pieces
115g/4oz cooked peeled prawns
salt and freshly ground black pepper
4 thick slices of French bread

1. Melt the butter in a large saucepan. Add the onion, garlic, carrot and leek and cook gently, for about 10 minutes, stirring occasionally, or until soft.

2. Add the tomatoes, stock and herbs. Bring to the boil, cover, reduce the heat and simmer for 10 minutes.

3. Add the fish and simmer very gently for 5 minutes.

4. Add the prawns and simmer very gently for 2 minutes. Season to taste with salt and pepper.

5. Toast the bread on both sides and place each piece in the base of a warmed bowl. Ladle the soup over the top and serve.

To microwave:
1. Put the butter into a large casserole and add the onion, garlic, carrot and leek. Cover and cook on High for 5 minutes, stirring once or twice, until very soft.

2. Stir in the tomatoes, stock and herbs. Cover and cook on High for about 5 minutes, or until the mixture comes to the boil, stirring once. Cook on Medium for 5 minutes.

3. Stir in the fish and cook on Medium for 3 minutes.

4. Stir in the prawns and cook on Medium for 2 minutes. Season to taste with salt and pepper.

5. As step 5.

Not suitable for slow-cooking.

Not suitable for freezing.

Crab Bisque

Plump fresh brown crabs are in season from summer through to spring and one makes a wonderful meal for four to six people, made into a rich soup with plenty of crusty bread and perhaps followed with some good cheese and a green salad.

Serves 4–6

1 large cooked brown crab
1 litre/1¾ pints Chicken Stock (see page 8) or Vegetable Stock (see page 4)
25g/1oz butter
1 onion, chopped
1 potato, peeled and diced
1 carrot, chopped
1 bay leaf
100ml/3½fl oz dry white wine
2 tbsp brandy
salt and freshly ground black pepper
150ml/¼ pint crème fraîche
a squeeze of lemon juice (optional)
a little milk, if necessary
a little chopped fresh parsley, to garnish

1. Remove all the meat from the crab, including the claws, keeping the white and dark meat separate. Put the crab shell and broken claws in a large saucepan with the stock. Bring to the boil, reduce the heat, cover and simmer for 40 minutes. Strain and stir in the brown crab meat.

2. Rinse out the saucepan, then melt the butter and fry the onion, potato and carrot gently, stirring, for 3–4 minutes until softening but not browning.

3. Add the bay leaf, white wine and brandy. Boil for a few minutes until reduced by half. Add the stock and a little salt and pepper, then simmer for 15 minutes until the vegetables are tender. While the soup is cooking, flake the white crab meat.

4. Discard the bay leaf and purée the soup in a blender or food processor, then return it to the pan. Stir in the crème fraîche and the white crab meat. Sharpen with a squeeze of lemon juice, if liked, and season to taste with salt and pepper. Thin, if necessary, with a little milk. Reheat gently, then ladle into warm bowls and serve garnished with chopped parsley.

Not suitable for microwaving.

To slow-cook:
1. As step 1 but put the ingredients in the slow-cooker. Add the hot stock. Cook on High for 2–3 hours or Low for 5–7 hours. Strain and return to the slow-cooker.

2. Cook the onion, potato and carrot in a saucepan with the butter. Continue as step 2. Add the bay leaf, wine and brandy and reduce by half as before.

3. Tip into the slow cooker, cover and cook on High for 1–2 hours or Low for 4–6 hours.

4. Flake the white crab meat and continue as step 4. Season to taste with salt and black pepper. If necessary return to the slow-cooker and leave on Low until ready to serve.

To freeze:
Cool and freeze at step 4 after puréeing and adding the crab meat but not the crème fraîche. To serve, thaw completely then add the crème fraîche and continue as step 4.

Clams and Pasta in Pernod and Saffron Broth

Clams are in season from autumn through spring but taste wonderful in this lovely saffron-based soup when the buds are out on the trees and there is the hope of pending summer in the air. You can, of course, cheat and use a can of clams but the flavour won't be anything like as good.

Serves 4

2 tbsp olive oil
1 onion or 2 shallots, finely chopped
1 large carrot, finely chopped
2 garlic cloves, crushed ·
900g/2lb clams in their shells, scrubbed
200ml/7fl oz dry cider
3 tbsp Pernod or other aniseed liqueur
900ml/1½ pints Fish Stock (see page 10) or Chicken Stock (see page 8)
a good pinch of saffron strands
2 tbsp chopped fresh parsley, plus a little extra for garnish
1 tbsp fresh thyme leaves
salt and freshly ground black pepper
100g/3½oz conchiglie pasta

1. Heat the oil in a large saucepan. Add the onion or shallots, the carrot and garlic. Stir, cover and cook over a gentle heat for 5 minutes to soften. Remove from the pan.

2. Meanwhile, wash and then pick over the clams. Discard any that are open, damaged or won't close when sharply tapped.

3. Tip the clams into the pan and add the cider. Bring to the boil, cover and shake the pan for 3–4 minutes until all the clams have opened. Discard any that remain closed.

4. Strain through a colander, saving the liquor. Keep 4 clams in their shells and remove the remainder. Return the liquor to the pan and add the onion or shallots, carrot, Pernod, stock, saffron, herbs and plenty of black pepper. Bring to the boil, add the pasta and boil for
15 minutes until tender.

5. Return the shelled clams to the pan and heat through. Season to taste with salt and pepper. Ladle into warm bowls and garnish with a little extra chopped parsley.

To microwave:
1. Put the oil, onion or shallots, carrot and garlic into a large casserole. Cook on High for 2 minutes, stirring once. Remove from the casserole.

2. Continue as step 2.

3. Put the clams and cider in the casserole. Cover and cook on High for about 3 minutes, stirring once, or until all the clams have opened. Discard any that remain closed.

4. Strain the pan juices through a colander and return them to the casserole. Continue as step 4 to cook on High for about 15 minutes until the pasta is tender.

5. As step 5.

Not suitable for slow-cooking.

To freeze:
Cool quickly after step 4, then add the clams and freeze. To serve, thaw completely, then reheat until piping hot.

Prawn Egg Flower Soup

The little North Atlantic prawns caught around Britain are in season from November until May so are delicious in spring. It's a bit fiddly peeling them but the shells make the stock utterly delicious. You could use sustainably fished shelled frozen prawns for quickness but the flavour won't be anything like as good.

Serves 4

400g/14oz unpeeled small prawns
1 bunch of spring onions
900ml/1½ pints Chicken Stock (see page 8)
1 tsp grated fresh root ginger
1 tbsp soy sauce
2 tbsp dry sherry
1 egg, beaten

1. Reserve 4 whole prawns for garnish. Peel the remaining prawns by pulling off the heads and tails then peeling off the body shell, starting from the underside where the legs are. Put the prawns in the fridge until needed. Put the prawn shells in a saucepan.

2. Trim the spring onions, chop and set aside. Put the trimmings in the saucepan with the prawn shells, and add the stock and ginger. Bring to the boil, reduce the heat, partially cover and simmer for 20 minutes. Strain the stock through a muslin-lined sieve (or use a new disposable kitchen cloth) and return it to the rinsed-out pan.

3. Reserve a little chopped green onion for garnish and add the remainder to the stock with the soy sauce and sherry. Bring to the boil and simmer for 3 minutes. Add the prawns and simmer for a further 1 minute.

4. Remove from the heat and pour the egg slowly in a thin stream through the prongs of fork so it solidifies in 'flowers'. Let the soup stand for 20 seconds to allow the egg to set, then ladle into warm soup bowls. Garnish each one with a reserved whole prawn on the side of the bowl and a sprinkling of the reserved spring onion.

To microwave:
1. As step 1.

2. Continue as step 2 but put the ingredients in a large bowl, cover and cook on High for 10 minutes, stirring occasionally.

3. Reserve a little chopped green onion for garnish and add the remainder to the stock with the soy sauce and sherry. Cook on High for 3 minutes, stirring once, then add the prawns and cook on High for 20 seconds. Add the egg to the hot soup as in step 4 above.

To slow-cook:
1. As step 1. Tip into the slow-cooker.

2. Continue as step 2 but add hot stock. Cover and cook on High for 2 hours or Low for 4–6 hours.

3. Continue as step 3 but add the prawns and leave on Low for 5 minutes. Add the egg and leave on Low for 5 minutes more before serving as step 3.

Not suitable for freezing.

Mussel Soup with Coconut and Coriander

Mussels are now farmed all year round but wild ones are available from autumn through to spring and are particularly delicious served this way when the clutches of winter melt away. Serve with plenty of warm crusty bread to mop up the fragrant juices. When cleaning the mussels, remember to discard any that are broken or that do not close when given a sharp tap.

Serves 4

25g/1oz plain flour
25g/1oz soft butter
150ml/¼ pint dry white wine
2 large garlic cloves, finely chopped
1 piece of lemon grass, finely chopped (see Cooks' tip) (optional)
450g/1lb small mussels, scrubbed and beards removed
600ml/1 pint Fish Stock (see page 10) or Vegetable Stock (see page 4)
165g/6oz can coconut cream
salt and freshly ground black pepper
4 tbsp chopped fresh coriander

1. Using a fork, work the flour into the butter until well blended. Leave on one side.

2. Put the wine, garlic and lemon grass (if using) into a large saucepan and bring to the boil. Add the mussels, cover and cook on a high heat for about 2 minutes, shaking the pan occasionally, until all the shells have opened.

3. Use a slotted spoon to transfer the mussels to a bowl. Reserve about 12 in their shells, then remove the remaining mussels from their shells, discarding any that have not opened.

4. Strain the pan juices through a fine sieve and return them to the rinsed-out pan. Add the stock and coconut cream, then season with salt and pepper. Bring to the boil, then simmer gently for 2–3 minutes.

5. Add the flour-and-butter mixture, one small piece at a time and stirring with a whisk, until the soup has thickened.

6. Return the mussels to the pan, including the 12 in their shells. Adjust the seasoning to taste, add the coriander and heat through gently. Serve the soup, dividing the mussels evenly between bowls.

To microwave:
1. As step 1.

2. Put the wine, garlic and lemon grass (if using) into a large casserole. Cook on High for 45 seconds. Stir in the mussels, cover and cook on High for about 4 minutes, stirring once, or until all the mussels have opened.

3. As step 3.

4. Strain the pan juices through a fine sieve and return them to the casserole. Add the stock and coconut cream, then season with salt and pepper. Cook on High for about 5 minutes or until the mixture comes to the boil, stirring once or twice.

5. As steps 5 and 6, heating through until the soup comes to the boil.

Not suitable for slow-cooking.

Not suitable for freezing.

COOKS' TIP: Herbs in oil
Look out for those handy small jars of fresh lemon grass and herbs packed in oil. Once opened they will keep in the fridge for up to six weeks.

Green Cabbage and Smoked Sausage Soup

Green cabbage is at its best in winter and into spring and, as early spring is often cold and damp, this is an ideal dish to warm up those chilly days. You can make it with white cabbage if you prefer.

Serves 4

15g/½oz butter
1 bunch of spring onions, chopped
1 carrot, thinly sliced
250g/9oz smoked pork ring, sliced
¼ hearty green cabbage, shredded, thick stump removed
1 large potato, peeled and cut into small dice
1 bouquet garni (see Cooks' tip on page 7)
2 tbsp chopped fresh parsley, plus extra for garnish
1 tbsp caraway seeds
2 tsp cider vinegar
1 litre/1¾ pints beef stock (see page 6)
salt and freshly ground black pepper

1. Melt the butter in a large saucepan, add the spring onions and carrot. Fry for 2 minutes, stirring.

2. Add the sausage and cook, stirring, for 1 minute.

3. Add all the remaining ingredients and bring to the boil. Reduce the heat, cover and simmer gently for 30 minutes or until everything is tender and the flavour is intense.

4. Season to taste with salt and pepper, if necessary. Discard the bouquet garni and ladle the soup into warm bowls. Garnish with a little extra chopped parsley before serving.

To microwave:

1. Put the butter, spring onions and carrot into a large casserole and cook on High for about 2 minutes until softened, stirring once.

2. Add all the remaining ingredients, but adding only half the hot stock. Cover and cook on High for 5 minutes until the cabbage is slightly wilted. Add the remaining stock and cook on High for about 20 minutes or until the vegetables are very soft, stirring once or twice.

3. As step 4.

To slow-cook:

1. As step 1. Tip into the slow-cooker and add the remaining ingredients, including the hot stock and seasoning.

2. Cover and cook on High for 4 hours or Low for 8 hours.

3. As step 4.

To freeze:

Cool and freeze at the end of step 3. To serve, thaw completely then continue as step 4.

Pork, Red Cabbage and Pear Soup

Red cabbage is at its best in late winter and early spring, overlapping beautifully with the best of the Conference pears, which are harvested in autumn but are still good throughout the winter and even into early spring. They make a welcome addition to fruit bowls and desserts as well as enhancing this hearty, lightly spiced sweet-and-sour soup.

Serves 4

225g/8oz lean pork shoulder or leg
1 tbsp sunflower oil
25g/1oz butter
1 onion, halved and thinly sliced
½ small red cabbage, shredded
400g/14oz can red kidney beans, drained
2 tbsp red wine vinegar
2 tbsp light soft brown sugar
1.2 litres/2 pints Chicken Stock (see page 8) or Vegetable Stock (see page 4)
½ tsp ground cinnamon
salt and freshly ground black pepper
a handful of raisins
a bay leaf
1 tbsp fennel seeds (optional)
2 Conference pears, peeled, cored and diced
a little thick, plain yogurt and some chopped fresh parsley, to garnish

1. Cut the pork into small strips no more than 2.5cm/1in long and the width of a little finger.

2. Heat the oil and butter in a large saucepan. Add the onion and fry, stirring, for 2 minutes to soften slightly. Add the pork and fry for a further 2 minutes, stirring.

3. Add the remaining ingredients except the pears and garnish. Bring to the boil, reduce the heat, partially cover and simmer gently for 40 minutes until really tender.

4. Stir in the pears and simmer for 2 minutes until the pieces are translucent but still hold their shape. Taste and re-season, if necessary. Discard the bay leaf. Ladle into warm soup bowls and garnish each with a spoonful of thick plain yogurt and a sprinkling of chopped parsley.

To microwave:
1. As step 1.

2. Put the oil, butter and onion in a large casserole and cook on High for 2 minutes, stirring once. Add the pork and cook on High for a further 1 minute.

3. Add the hot stock and the remaining ingredients except the pears and garnish. Cover and cook on High for about 5 minutes or until the mixture comes to the boil, stirring once. Stir, cover and cook on Medium for about 25 minutes, or until the pork is tender, stirring once or twice.

4. Add the pears and cook on High for 1 minute until the pears are translucent but still holding their shape. Serve as step 4.

To slow-cook:
1. As step 1.

2. Continue as step 2.

3. Tip the pork and onions into the slow-cooker. Add hot stock and the remaining ingredients except the pears and garnish. Cover and cook on High for 3 hours or Low for 6 hours.

4. Continue as step 4 but cook on High for 5 minutes.

To freeze:
Cool, then freeze at the end of step 3. To serve, thaw completely, reheat then add the pears and continue as step 4.

Sparkling Pink Rhubarb and Ginger Soup

The delicate, tender, pink forced rhubarb is in season from February to April. Try serving it in this glorious, refreshing, pink frothy soup to round off any special-occasion meal. Don't over-sweeten the rhubarb as the ginger ale adds enough sweetness and you want a nice tang to the soup.

Serves 6

450g/1lb forced rhubarb, trimmed and cut into short lengths
40g/1½oz caster sugar
2.5cm/1in piece of fresh root ginger, peeled and lightly crushed but left whole
5 tbsp water
about 200ml/7fl oz ginger ale, well chilled

To serve:
thick vanilla yogurt

1. Put the rhubarb in a large saucepan with the sugar, ginger and water. Bring to the boil, cover, reduce the heat and simmer gently for 5 minutes, stirring occasionally until thick and pulpy. Remove the lid and boil rapidly for 1–2 minutes to evaporate most of the juice.

2. Discard the crushed piece of ginger, then purée the rhubarb in a blender or food processor.

3. Tip into a plastic container with a lid, cool, cover and chill until ready to serve.

4. Ladle the chilled purée into open soup plates. Pour the sparkling ginger ale over and stir well. Quickly add a spoonful of thick vanilla yogurt to the centre of each bowl and serve straight away.

To microwave:
1. Put the rhubarb in a large casserole, spreading it out evenly. Add the sugar and ginger and only 1 tablespoon water. Cover and cook on High for about 5 minutes, or until thick and pulpy, stirring occasionally. Remove the lid and microwave a little longer to evaporate most of the juice.

2. As steps 2–4.

To slow-cook:
1. Put the rhubarb in the slow-cooker with the sugar and ginger and add 5 tablespoons hot water, rather than cold. Cover and cook on High for 1–2 hours or Low for 3–4 hours. You will then need to tip it in a saucepan to boil rapidly to evaporate the juice.

2. As steps 2–4.

To freeze:
Cool and freeze at the end of step 3. To serve, thaw completely, then continue as step 4.

5 Summer Soups

Summer soups should be light and sumptuous. They may be cool and refreshing, such as a light fruit soup for dessert or to start a special meal; crisp and fresh, such as a no-cook gazpacho or a chilled watercress and orange soup; or warm and packed with flavour, such as gorgeous, golden sweetcorn. Or a French-style fish soup. Many will make a tempting light lunch or supper, others need a little something to round off the meal, such as a light summer salad. All these recipes make the most of the abundance of fresh, seasonable produce available throughout the summer. The choice is almost overwhelming and utterly delicious!

Gazpacho

No cooking here! This is a soup made from fresh summer salad ingredients and thickened with breadcrumbs. Serve it with croûtons and extra vegetables – tomatoes, cucumber, peppers and onions, all cut into tiny pieces.

Serves 4–6

675g/1½lb ripe tomatoes, skinned, deseeded and chopped (see Cooks' tip page 69)
1 small cucumber, skinned, deseeded and chopped
1 green or red pepper, deseeded and chopped
6 spring onions, thinly sliced
2 large garlic cloves, crushed
2 tbsp olive oil
2 tbsp red or white wine vinegar
115g/4oz fresh white breadcrumbs
1 tsp caster sugar
salt and freshly ground black pepper
600ml/1 pint cold Chicken Stock (see page 8), plus extra if necessary

1. Put the tomatoes in a large bowl and add the cucumber, pepper, onions, garlic, oil, vinegar, breadcrumbs and sugar. Season with salt and pepper and mix well. Leave to stand for 10 minutes, stirring once or twice.

2. Stir in the cold stock. Tip into a food processor or blender and purée until smooth. If necessary, add extra stock until the consistency is right for serving.

3. Chill for 2 hours or more.

To freeze:
Freeze at the end of step 3. To serve, thaw and serve chilled.

Chilled Avocado and Spring Onion Soup

Try adding a splash of dry white wine to the chilled soup, just before serving.

Serves 4

1 bunch of spring onions
2 ripe avocados
finely grated zest and juice of 1 small lemon
150ml/¼ pint double cream
600ml/1 pint cold Chicken Stock (see page 8) or Vegetable Stock (see page 4)
salt and freshly ground black pepper

1. Chop the onions, reserving some of the green tops for garnish. Put them into a food processor or blender.

2. Halve the avocados, remove the stones and spoon the flesh into the processor. Add the lemon rind and juice and purée until smooth. Add the cream and purée again.

3. Rub through a fine sieve into a large bowl to remove any stringy bits. Gradually whisk in the cold stock and season to taste with salt and pepper. Chill until required.

4. Serve garnished with the reserved chopped spring onion tops.

Not suitable for freezing.

Chilled Cucumber and Mint Soup

Cooling cucumbers are prolific in summer – especially the outdoor ridged varieties, which are particularly good for this recipe as they have a little more flavour than the hothouse ones (though they can be used instead, of course). This is another recipe that needs no cooking. It looks pretty served in glass bowls with one or two ice cubes dropped into each one. Serve it with crisp savoury biscuits or Melba Toast (see page 19).

Serves 6

2 ridge cucumbers
6 spring onions, sliced
15g/½oz fresh mint leaves, plus extra to garnish
600ml/1 pint cold Chicken Stock (see page 8)
1 tsp caster sugar
1 tbsp white wine vinegar
150ml/¼ pint double cream
150ml/¼ pint thick Greek-style plain yogurt
salt and freshly ground black pepper

1. Top and tail the cucumbers and halve lengthways. Scoop out and discard the seeds and roughly chop the flesh.

2. Put the chopped cucumber into a food processor or blender. Add the onions, mint, stock, sugar and vinegar. Purée until very smooth.

3. Transfer the mixture to a large bowl and gently whisk in the cream and yogurt. Season to taste with salt and pepper.

4. Chill until required. Serve garnished with mint leaves.

Not suitable for freezing.

Chilled Minted Pea Soup

The pea season is throughout summer into autumn. This tasty recipe is the ideal way to use up peas that may have been left in the pod a little too long so aren't quite as sweet and tender as you would like to serve as a vegetable. Make sure they are completely tender before puréeing so they give a lovely smooth-textured soup.

Serves 4–6

8 spring onions, sliced
175g/6oz fresh, shelled peas
175g/6oz potatoes, peeled and thinly sliced
450ml/¾ pint Vegetable Stock (see page 4)
450ml/¾ pint milk
2 tsp concentrated mint sauce
salt and freshly ground black pepper

To serve:
150ml/¼ pint Greek-style yogurt
snipped fresh chives

1. Put the onions, peas, potatoes and stock into a pan. Bring to the boil, then cover, reduce the heat and simmer gently for about 15 minutes, or until the vegetables are very soft.

2. Leave to cool slightly, then tip into a food processor or blender and purée until smooth. Add the milk and mint sauce and purée again. Season to taste with salt and pepper.

3. Cool, cover and chill for several hours.

4. Just before serving, lightly stir in the yogurt. Serve sprinkled with snipped chives.

To microwave:
1. Put the onions, peas, potatoes and hot stock into a large casserole. Cover and cook on High for about 12 minutes, stirring once or twice, or until the vegetables are soft.

2. As steps 2–4.

To slow-cook:
1. Put all the ingredients in the crockpot with the hot stock. Cover and cook on High for 2 hours or Low for 4–6 hours.

2. As steps 2–4.

To freeze:
Cool and freeze at the end of step 2. To serve, continue as steps 3 and 4.

Chilled Beetroot Soup

A splash of vodka added just before serving adds an exciting kick to this delicious summer soup when serving for a special occasion. Look out for golden beetroot or the stripy Chioggia varieties. They make a delicious and colourful alternative to the conventional red beets. You can leave the vegetables in the soup if you prefer.

Serves 4–6

1kg/2¼lb beetroot
1 large onion, finely chopped
1.2 litres/2 pints Chicken Stock (see page 8) or Vegetable Stock (see page 4)
salt and freshly ground black pepper
1 tsp caster sugar
2 tbsp red or white wine vinegar

To serve:
soured cream or thick plain yogurt
snipped fresh chives

1. Peel and coarsely grate the beetroot. Put into a pan and add the onion and stock. Season with salt and pepper and the sugar. Bring to the boil, cover, reduce the heat and simmer gently for about 45 minutes.

2. Strain, discarding the vegetables. Stir the vinegar into the soup and season to taste with salt and pepper.

3. Cool, then chill until ready to serve topped with a generous spoonful of soured cream or yogurt and some chives.

To microwave:
1. Peel and coarsely grate the beetroot. Put into a large casserole and add the onion and half the hot stock. Season with salt and pepper and the sugar.

2. Cover and cook on High for about 5 minutes or until the mixture comes to the boil, stirring once. Continue to cook on Medium for about 20 minutes, stirring once or twice.

3. Stir in the remaining stock, leave to stand for 5–10 minutes, then continue as steps 2 and 3.

To slow-cook:
1. Peel and coarsely grate the beetroot into the slow-cooker. Continue as step 1. Cover and cook on High for 2–3 hours or Low for 5–7 hours.

2. As steps 2 and 3.

To freeze:
Cool then freeze at step 2. To serve, thaw, then serve cold garnished as step 3.

Roasted Plum Tomato Soup

If you cannot get plum tomatoes, use any ripe variety. This is especially good served with freshly baked or toasted ciabatta.

Serves 4

900g/2lb ripe plum tomatoes, halved lengthways
3 tbsp olive oil
2 large garlic cloves, finely chopped
2 tbsp chopped fresh thyme or 1 tbsp dried
900ml/1½ pints Chicken Stock (see page 8) or Vegetable Stock (see page 4)
salt and freshly ground black pepper
a handful of fresh basil leaves, torn

1. Preheat the oven to 200°C/Gas 6.

2. Arrange the tomatoes, cut-side up, on a baking sheet. Drizzle over 2 tablespoons olive oil. Cook in the oven for about 45 minutes, or until the tomatoes are soft and brown.

3. Tip the tomatoes, with any juices, into a food processor or blender and blend until slightly chunky. (If you prefer a very smooth soup, purée for longer, then rub it through a fine sieve.)

4. Heat the remaining oil in a large saucepan, add the garlic and cook gently for 1–2 minutes without browning it. Stir in the tomatoes, thyme and stock. Bring to the boil, reduce the heat and simmer gently for 15–20 minutes. Season to taste with salt and pepper.

5. Just before serving, stir in a generous amount of torn basil leaves.

To microwave:
1. As steps 1 and 2.

2. Put the remaining 1 tbsp oil into a large casserole. Stir in the garlic and cook on High for 20 seconds. Add the tomatoes, thyme and half the hot stock. Cover and cook on High for about 10 minutes, stirring once or twice.

3. Stir in the remaining stock and continue as steps 4 and 5.

To slow-cook:
1. As steps 1 and 2.

2. Put all the ingredients in the crockpot and cook on High for 1–2 hours or Low for 4–6 hours. Season and serve as step 5.

To freeze:
Cool and freeze at the end of step 4. To serve, reheat gently then continue as step 5.

Watercress and Orange Soup

Watercress is now available most of the year but this is the classic, summer soup. It looks beautiful garnished with thin strips of orange zest (cooked in boiling water for 2–3 minutes until tender) in addition to the watercress. For traditional plain soup, simply omit the orange. This soup is also good served chilled.

Serves 6

2 bunches of watercress
25g/1oz butter
1 onion, finely chopped
1 potato, peeled and cut into small pieces
900ml/1½ pints Chicken Stock (see page 8) or Vegetable Stock (see page 4)
300ml/½ pint milk
1 orange
salt and freshly ground black pepper

To serve:
a little single cream

1. Reserve a few sprigs of watercress for garnish, then roughly chop the rest.

2. Melt the butter in a large saucepan, add the onion and cook gently for about 5 minutes, stirring occasionally, until soft but not brown.

3. Stir in the watercress and potato. Add the stock and season with salt and pepper. Bring to the boil, reduce the heat and simmer gently for about 15 minutes until the potato is very soft.

4. Leave to cool slightly, then add the milk. Tip into a food processor or blender and purée until smooth. Return the soup to the pan.

5. Finely grate half the zest from the orange and squeeze the juice from both halves. Add to the pan and season to taste with salt and pepper.

6. Reheat gently. Serve each bowl with a little cream spooned over the top and garnish with the reserved watercress.

To microwave:
1. As step 1.

2. Put the butter and onion into a large casserole and cook on High for about 3 minutes until soft, stirring once.

3. Stir in the watercress and potato. Add half the hot stock and season with salt and pepper. Cover and cook on High for about 10 minutes, or until the potato is very soft, stirring once or twice.

4. Add the remaining stock, then continue as steps 4–6.

To slow-cook:
1. Melt the butter in a frying pan and cook the onion gently for 5 minutes, stirring occasionally until soft but not brown.

2. Tip the sautéed onion into the crockpot and add the watercress and potato.

3. Pour on the hot stock, season with salt and pepper and cook on High for 1–2 hours or Low for 4–6 hours.

4. Leave to cool slightly, then add the milk. Purée as step 4, then return to the slow-cooker on High and continue as steps 5 and 6.

To freeze:
Cool and freeze at step 5. To serve, thaw, then reheat and garnish as step 6.

Herbed Tomato Soup with Rice

This recipe is just as good when the rice is replaced with fine
vermicelli. If you don't have a glut of tomatoes, or time is short, you
can cheat and use a 400g/14oz can chopped tomatoes for half of them
but it's worth having some chopped fresh ones to add at the end.

Serves 6

1 tbsp olive oil
1 onion, finely chopped
1 large garlic clove, finely chopped
8 ripe tomatoes, skinned and chopped
1 tbsp tomato purée
900ml/1½ pints Vegetable Stock (see page 4)
1 tsp dried oregano, or 1½ tbsp chopped fresh
1 tbsp sugar
salt and freshly ground black pepper
50g/1¾oz long-grain rice

1. Put the oil, onion and garlic into a large saucepan and cook
gently for about 5 minutes, stirring occasionally, until soft but not
brown.

2. Stir in the half the tomatoes (including all the seeds and juice),
the tomato purée, stock, oregano and sugar. Bring to the boil,
reduce the heat, cover and simmer gently for about 10 minutes.
Season to taste with salt and pepper.

3. Leave to cool slightly, then tip the mixture into a food processor
or blender and purée until smooth.

4. Return the puréed mixture to the pan and stir in the rice. Bring
to the boil, then simmer gently for about 10 minutes or until the
rice is just tender.

5. Stir in the reserved fresh chopped tomatoes, season to taste with
salt and pepper and serve.

To microwave:
1. Put the oil, onion and garlic into a large casserole. Cook on High for about 3 minutes until soft.

2. Stir in half the tomatoes, as in step 2, half the hot stock, the oregano, sugar and tomato purée. Cover and cook on High for about 5 minutes, stirring once. Add the remaining stock and season with salt and pepper.

3. Continue as step 3.

4. Return the puréed mixture to the casserole and stir in the rice. Cook, uncovered, on High for about 10 minutes or until the rice is just tender, stirring once or twice.

5. Stir in the fresh tomatoes, adjust the seasoning if necessary and serve.

Not suitable for slow-cooking.

To freeze:
Cool and freeze at the end of step 3. To serve, reheat gently, then continue as steps 4 and 5.

COOKS' TIP: Skinning tomatoes
*To skin fresh tomatoes, make a knick in the skin of each with
a sharp knife. Pour over sufficient boiling water to cover
them and leave to stand for 30 seconds. Drain them and
the skins will peel off easily.*

Grilled Red Pepper Soup

Peppers are at their best at the height of summer. Grilling them first gives the soup a lovely smoky flavour. Red peppers have the sweetest flavour, though orange or yellow ones could be substituted. If you like spice, try adding a teaspoon or two of harissa paste to the mixture.

Serves 6

3 large red peppers
1 tbsp olive oil
1 red onion, finely chopped
2 garlic cloves, finely chopped
1 tbsp caster sugar
400g/14oz can chopped tomatoes
1 litre/1¾ pints Chicken Stock (see page 8) or Vegetable Stock (see page 4)
4 tbsp torn fresh basil
salt and freshly ground black pepper

To serve:
crème fraîche
a few fresh basil leaves

1. Preheat the grill. Put the whole peppers about 7.5–10cm/3–4in away from the heat. Grill them, turning frequently, until their skins are black and blistered. Carefully put them into a plastic bag and leave to cool.

2. Peel the skins off the cooled peppers, cut them open and collect the juices. Remove and discard the stalk ends, seeds and white membrane, then cut the flesh into small pieces.

3. Put the oil, onion, garlic and sugar into a large saucepan. Cook gently for about 5 minutes, stirring occasionally, until soft and beginning to turn golden brown. Add the tomatoes, peppers with their reserved juices, stock and basil. Bring to the boil, reduce the heat and simmer gently for about 15 minutes.

4. Leave to cool slightly, then tip the mixture into a food processor or blender and purée until smooth. Season to taste with salt and pepper.

5. Reheat gently, then serve topped with a spoonful of crème fraîche and a few basil leaves.

To microwave:
1. As steps 1 and 2.

2. Put the oil, onion, garlic and sugar into a large casserole. Cover and cook on High for about 3 minutes until soft, stirring once. Add the tomatoes, peppers with their reserved juices, basil and half the hot stock. Cover and cook on High for about 5 minutes, or until the mixture comes to the boil. Stir, then cook on High for a further 5 minutes.

3. Add the remaining stock, then continue as step 4.

4. As step 5.

To slow-cook:
1. Prepare as steps 1–3. When the onion is turning golden brown, tip the mixture into the crockpot. Add the tomatoes, peppers with their reserved juices, hot stock and basil.

2. Cover and cook on High for 2 hours or Low for 4–6 hours.

3. Continue as step 4. Serve immediately or tip back in the crock pot and leave on Low until ready to serve garnished as step 5.

To freeze:
Cool and freeze at the end of step 4. To serve, continue as step 5.

Lettuce and Petits Pois Soup

This recipe is ideal for using up lettuce that is beginning to bolt in the summer garden or the outer leaves of lettuces when you've used the hearts for salads or for braising. You can make a version of this using the pea pods, when you've shelled the peas to serve as a vegetable. (You'll need about 350g/12oz unshelled peas to get the right amount of pods to cook with the lettuce.) When puréed, you'll need to sieve the soup to remove the fibrous parts of the pods.

Serves 4

25g/1oz butter
1 onion, finely chopped
225g/8oz lettuce leaves, shredded
175g/6oz fresh, shelled or frozen petits pois
1 tbsp plain flour
750ml/1¼ pints Vegetable Stock (see page 4)
salt and freshly ground black pepper
200g/7oz crème fraîche
2 tbsp chopped fresh herbs, such as mint, parsley or coriander

1. Melt the butter in a large saucepan, add the onion and cook gently for 2–3 minutes until soft but not brown.

2. Stir in the lettuce and petits pois and cook gently for 2–3 minutes, stirring, until the lettuce has wilted. Stir in the flour, then gradually add the stock. Bring to the boil, stirring, then reduce the heat, cover and simmer gently for about 10 minutes until everything is tender.

3. Leave to cool slightly, then tip into a food processor or blender and purée until smooth. Season to taste with salt and pepper.

4. Stir in the crème fraîche and herbs. Reheat gently without allowing the soup to boil.

To microwave
1. Put the butter and onion into a large casserole, cover and cook on High for 2 minutes until soft.

2. Stir in the lettuce and petit pois and cook on High for 2 minutes until the lettuce has wilted. Stir in the flour, then gradually add the hot stock. Cook on High for about 5 minutes, stirring occasionally, until the mixture comes to the boil. Cover and cook on Medium for about 10 minutes, stirring once or twice.

3. Continue as steps 3–4.

Not suitable for slow-cooking.

To freeze:
Cool and freeze at the end of step 3. To serve, reheat gently and complete as step 4.

Chicken Chowder

I like to use new potatoes in this recipe. Alternatively, use a maincrop variety that will hold its shape, such as Estima, Cara or Desirée. Serve it with crusty rolls.

Serves 4–6

25g/1oz butter
1 onion, finely chopped
1 small head of fennel, finely chopped
225g/8oz potatoes (preferably new), scrubbed and diced
1 large boneless chicken breast, skinned and cut into small cubes
4 boneless chicken thighs, skinned and cut into small cubes
600ml/1 pint Chicken Stock (see page 8)
175g/6oz fresh sweetcorn kernels from 2 large cobs (see page 86) or use frozen
600ml/1 pint milk
salt and freshly ground black pepper
snipped fresh chives, to garnish

1. Melt the butter in a large saucepan and stir in the onion, fennel and potatoes. Cook gently for about 5 minutes, stirring occasionally, until soft but not brown. Add the chicken and cook, stirring, for a few minutes until the chicken is no longer pink.

2. Stir in the stock and sweetcorn. Bring to the boil, cover and reduce the heat. Simmer gently for about 15 minutes, stirring once or twice, or until the chicken and potatoes are tender but still hold their shape.

3. Add the milk and reheat gently. Ladle into warm bowls, season and garnish with snipped chives.

To microwave:
1. Put the butter, onion, fennel and potatoes into a large casserole. Cover and cook on High for about 5 minutes, stirring once, until soft.

2. Stir in the chicken, then add the hot stock and sweetcorn. Cover and cook on High for about 5 minutes, or until the mixture comes to the boil, stirring once. Continue cooking on Medium for 5–10 minutes, stirring once or twice, until the chicken and potatoes are tender but still hold their shape.

3. Add the milk and season with salt and pepper to taste. Cook on High for about 2 minutes, or until piping hot. Serve as step 3.

To slow-cook:
1. Prepare as step 1 and tip into the crockpot.

2. Add the hot stock and remaining ingredients.

3. Cover and cook on High for 2–3 hours or Low for 5–7 hours.

4. Continue as step 3.

Not suitable for freezing.

Curried Aubergine and Coconut Soup

Aubergines are in season from right through summer into autumn. Considering this is a hot, spicy soup, it is remarkably light and perfect served with some naan breads at lunchtime. Aubergines used to have to be salted before use to remove their bitter juices but modern strains don't require this.

Serves 4

2 tbsp sunflower oil
1 onion, chopped
1 garlic clove
1 tbsp madras curry paste
1 large aubergine, cut in fairly small dice
200ml/7fl oz thick plain yogurt
900ml/1½ pints Vegetable Stock (see page 4) or Chicken Stock (see page 8)
2 tbsp tomato purée
165g/5¾oz can coconut cream
100g/3½oz fresh, shelled or frozen peas
50g/1¾oz desiccated coconut
½ tsp caster sugar
salt and freshly ground black pepper
2 tbsp chopped fresh coriander

1. Heat the oil in a large saucepan. Add the onion and garlic and fry gently, stirring, for about 4 minutes until lightly golden. Add the curry paste and fry for 30 seconds. Stir in the aubergine and yogurt and bring to the boil. Reduce the heat and cook for about 5 minutes until the mixture is thick (it will curdle at first).

2. Blend in the stock, tomato purée and coconut cream. Add the peas, coconut and sugar. Bring back to the boil, stirring, reduce the heat, partially cover and simmer for 15–20 minutes until the aubergine is really tender but still holds its shape. Season to taste with salt and pepper and add half the coriander.

3. Ladle into warm soup bowls and serve garnished with the remaining coriander.

To microwave:
1. Put the oil, onion and garlic in a large casserole and cook on High for 2 minutes, stirring once. Add the curry paste and cook on High for 15 seconds. Add the aubergine and yogurt and cook on High for 2 minutes until the mixture is thick, stirring once.

2. Continue as step 2, adding hot stock. Cover and cook on High for 5 minutes or until the aubergine is tender, stirring once.

3. As step 3.

To slow-cook:
1. As step 1 but tip the curry paste and onion mixture into the slow-cooker and stir in the aubergine, yogurt and coconut. Cover and cook on High for 1 hours or Low for 2–3 hours.

2. Continue as step 2 but add hot stock. Cover and cook on High for 1 hour or Low for 2–3 hours.

3. Continue as step 3.

To freeze:
Cool then freeze at the end of step 2. To serve, thaw completely, then reheat thoroughly and garnish as step 3.

Chanterelle Mushroom Soup with Brandy

Chanterelle mushrooms appear from early summer – way before the majority of woodland and field specimens. They are now cultivated too so there's no excuse for not enjoying them in this special occasion soup. Omit the cream if preferred.

Serves 6

25g/1oz butter
1 onion, finely chopped
300g/11oz chanterelle mushrooms, wiped and halved or quartered if large
100g/3½oz chestnut mushrooms, sliced
900ml/1½ pints Chicken Stock (see page 8) or Vegetable Stock (see page 4)
2 tbsp brandy
1 tbsp soy sauce
1 bouquet garni (see Cooks' tip on page 7)
salt and freshly ground black pepper
2 tbsp plain flour
1 tsp tomato purée
3 tbsp double cream
a little chopped fresh parsley, to garnish

1. Melt the butter in a large saucepan, add the onion and fry gently for 2 minutes, stirring. Stir in the mushrooms and cook for 2 minutes, stirring.

2. Add the stock, brandy, soy sauce and bouquet garni. Season lightly with salt and pepper. Bring to the boil, reduce the heat, partially cover and simmer gently for 20 minutes until rich and full of flavour.

3. Blend the flour with enough water to make a paste and tomato purée. Stir into the soup and simmer gently, stirring, for 2 minutes to thicken. Discard the bouquet garni, stir in the cream and season to taste with salt and pepper.

4. Ladle into warm open soup plates and sprinkle with a little chopped parsley before serving.

To microwave:
1. Put the butter and onion in a large casserole and cook on High for 1 minute. Stir, add the mushrooms and cook on High for 2 minutes, stirring once.

2. Continue as step 2, adding hot stock. Cover and cook on High for about 7 minutes or until the onions and mushrooms are really tender, stirring once or twice.

3. Continue as step 3 but cook on High for 2 minutes, or until thickened. Continue as steps 3 and 4.

To slow-cook:
1. As step 1. Tip into the slow-cooker.

2. Continue as step 2 but add hot stock. Before cooking, blend the flour with the water and tomato purée and stir in. Cover and cook on High for 2 hours or Low for 4 hours.

3. Continue as step 3. Season to taste with salt and pepper. Stir in the cream, cover and leave on Low for a couple of minutes to heat through.

4. As step 4.

To freeze:
Cool, then freeze at the end of step 2. To serve, thaw completely, then reheat thoroughly, stir in the cream and garnish as step 3.

Broad Bean and Spinach Soup

Quite a lot of broad beans you buy in the shops have been allowed to get too big so the centres have already become floury and the skins tough. Even these beans, which are not as sweet as we would like, still make a fabulous soup, especially when paired with spinach.

Serves 4

15g/½oz butter
1 onion, chopped
1 large potato, peeled and diced
350g/12oz spinach leaves
225g/8oz fresh, shelled broad beans
1 tbsp chopped fresh sage
salt and freshly ground black pepper
a good grating of nutmeg
900ml/1½ pints Chicken Stock (see page 8) or Vegetable Stock (see page 4)
120ml/4fl oz single cream, plus a little extra for garnish (optional)

1. Melt the butter in a large saucepan and fry the onion very gently, stirring, for 2 minutes to soften slightly but not brown.

2. Add all the remaining ingredients except the cream. Bring to the boil, reduce the heat and simmer gently for 30 minutes.

3. Cool slightly, then purée in a blender or food processor. Rub through a sieve, if you like, to remove any tough skins. Return to the rinsed-out pan. Stir in the cream, taste and re-season with more nutmeg, salt and pepper, if necessary. Reheat but do not boil. Ladle into warm soup bowls and add an extra swirl of cream, if using.

To microwave:
1. Put the butter and onion in a large casserole and cook on High for 1–2 minutes, stirring once.

2. Continue as step 2, adding half the hot stock. Cover and cook on High for 5 minutes until brought to the boil, stirring once, then cook on Medium for 10–15 minutes until the beans are really tender.

3. Add the remaining hot stock, then continue as step 3. Return the soup to the microwave to reheat for 1 minute on Medium but do not boil. Garnish as step 3.

To slow-cook:
1. As step 1. Tip into the slow-cooker.

2. Continue as step 2 but add hot stock. Cover and cook on High for 2 hours or Low for 4–6 hours.

3. Continue as step 3. Tip back in the slow-cooker and leave on Low for at least 5 minutes to heat through. Garnish as step 3.

To freeze:
Cool then freeze at step 3 before adding the cream. To serve, thaw completely, then reheat thoroughly, stir in the cream, season with salt and pepper, then serve as step 3.

Ratatouille Potage

All the wonderful Mediterranean vegetables burst into life in summer and we grow them all in the UK now. Adding a handful of toasted pine nuts just before serving adds a delicious crunch but you can omit if you prefer.

Serves 4–6

3 tbsp olive oil

1 red onion, chopped

1 garlic clove, chopped

1 aubergine, cut in small dice

1 courgette, cut in small dice

1 red pepper, deseeded and cut in small dice

4 ripe tomatoes, chopped

1 litre/1¾ pints Vegetable Stock (see page 4)

3 tbsp tomato purée

1 tsp dried oregano

1 tsp caster sugar

salt and freshly ground black pepper

2 tbsp torn fresh basil

freshly grated Parmesan cheese, to serve

1. Heat the oil in a large saucepan. Add the onion and garlic and fry gently, stirring, for 2–3 minutes until soft but not brown.

2. Add the remaining vegetables and toss gently for 1 minute. Add the stock, tomato purée, oregano and sugar and season with salt and pepper. Bring to the boil, reduce the heat, partially cover and simmer gently for 20 minutes until everything is really tender.

3. Season to taste with salt and pepper. Stir in the torn basil and ladle into warm bowls. Serve with plenty of freshly grated Parmesan to sprinkle over.

To microwave:
1. Put the oil, onion and garlic in a large casserole and cook on High for 2 minutes, stirring once.

2. Continue as step 2, adding half the hot stock. Cook on High for 10 minutes or until the vegetables are tender, stirring occasionally.

3. As step 3.

To slow-cook:
1. As step 1. Tip into the slow-cooker.

2. Continue as step 2 but add hot stock. Cover and cook on High for 2 hours or Low for 4–6 hours.

3. As step 3.

To freeze:
Cool then freeze at step 3 before adding the basil. To serve, thaw completely, then reheat thoroughly and add the torn basil. Serve as step 3.

Green Bean and Tomato Soup with Tapenade

You can use the thin French beans for this soup, which come into season in early summer. Alternatively, you can try it with runner beans, which are at their best from mid-summer, just removing the strings, then cutting the beans across into 5mm/¼in strips.

Serves 4

2 tbsp olive oil
1 large onion, finely chopped
1 large garlic clove, chopped
225g/8oz French beans, topped, tailed and chopped into 1cm/½in lengths
3 beefsteak tomatoes, skinned and chopped
150ml/5fl oz dry cider
750ml/1¼ pints Vegetable Stock (see page 4)
2 tbsp tomato purée
½ tsp caster sugar
1 tbsp chopped fresh rosemary
salt and freshly ground black pepper (optional)
1 tbsp cornflour
2 tbsp water

For the tapenade:
2 anchovy fillets
1 tbsp pickled capers, rinsed and drained
40g/1½oz stoned black olives
a handful of fresh parsley, chopped
1 tbsp olive oil
salt and freshly ground black pepper
lemon juice

1. Heat the oil in a large saucepan. Add the onion and garlic and fry gently, stirring, for 2 minutes to soften.

2. Add the remaining soup ingredients, except the cornflour and water, and bring to the boil. Reduce the heat, partially cover and simmer gently for 15 minutes until the beans are really tender.

3. Blend the cornflour with the water and stir into the soup. Bring to the boil and cook for 1 minute, stirring until thickened. Season to taste with salt and pepper, if necessary.

4. Meanwhile put the tapenade ingredients, except the olive oil and lemon juice, in a small food processor and chop finely (alternatively chop everything finely with a large knife). Blend in the olive oil, season with pepper and sharpen to taste with lemon juice.

5. Ladle the soup into warm bowls and top each one with a spoonful of tapenade.

To microwave:
1. Put the oil, onion and garlic in a large casserole and cook on High for 2 minutes, stirring once.

2. Continue as step 2, adding half the hot stock. Cook on High for 10 minutes or until the vegetables are really tender.

3. Continue as step 3. Microwave on High for 2 minutes until thickened and clear, stirring once or twice.

4. Continue as step 4 and 5.

To slow-cook:
1. As step 1. Tip into the slow-cooker.

2. Continue as step 2 but add hot stock. Cover and cook on High for 2 hours or Low for 4–6 hours.

3. Continue as step 3 but when the blended cornflour is stirred into the soup, cover and cook on High for 15 minutes until thickened.

4. As steps 4 and 5.

To freeze:
Cool, then freeze at the end of step 2. To serve, thaw completely then reheat thoroughly and continue from step 3.

Sweetcorn Soup

Fresh sweetcorn has a short season in late summer/early autumn. It is very easy to prepare. To remove the kernels, simply hold the cob upright on a board and with a sharp knife cut down the length of the cob all round to slice them off. Choose cobs with pale yellow kernels. If they are deep golden, the sugar has already started to turn to starch and they won't be as sweet.

Serves 4

25g/1oz butter
1 onion, finely chopped
450g/1lb sweetcorn from about 4–5 cobs or use frozen
600ml/1 pint Chicken Stock (see page 8) or Vegetable Stock (see page 4)
600ml/1 pint milk
salt and freshly ground black pepper

To serve:
double cream
Croûtons (see page 16)
chopped fresh parsley

1. Put the butter and onion into a large saucepan and cook gently for about 5 minutes until soft but not brown, stirring once.

2. Stir in the sweetcorn and stock. Bring to the boil, cover and reduce the heat. Simmer gently for about 20 minutes until the sweetcorn is very soft.

3. Leave to cool slightly, then tip the mixture into a food processor or blender and purée until smooth. Rub through a sieve, pressing the residue to squeeze out all the liquid. Return the liquid to the pan.

4. Tip the sweetcorn residue back into the processor or blender and add the milk. Purée for a minute or two. Now rub this mixture through the sieve, again pressing it to squeeze out all the juice. Add the liquid to the pan and season to taste with salt and pepper. Discard the residue.

5. Reheat gently and serve each bowl with a swirl of cream, a spoonful of croûtons and some chopped parsley.

To microwave:
1. Put the butter and onion into a large casserole. Cover and cook on High for about 3 minutes, stirring once, until soft.

2. Stir in the sweetcorn and stock. Cover and cook on High for about 15 minutes, stirring once, until the sweetcorn is very soft.

3. As steps 3–5.

Not suitable for slow-cooking.

To freeze:
Cool, then freeze at the end of step 4. To serve, continue as step 5.

COOKS' TIP: Sweetcorn
*To use canned sweetcorn in place of frozen, drain two
300g/11oz cans.*

Spiced Courgette Soup

Courgettes are prolific through the summer. This is a good way to use up those that have got a little large (as can happen if you have a glut in the garden) though any are, of course, fine. The soup is lovely served hot or chilled. Garnish it with some thin slices of courgette, either blanched or lightly fried in butter.

Serves 4

25g/1oz butter
1 onion, finely chopped
1 large garlic clove, crushed
1 tsp ground cumin
1 tsp ground coriander
350g/12oz courgettes, sliced
1 potato, peeled and sliced
450ml/¾ pint Chicken Stock (see page 8) or Vegetable Stock (see page 4)
300ml/½ pint milk
salt and freshly ground black pepper

1. Melt the butter in a large saucepan and add the onion and garlic. Cook gently for about 5 minutes, stirring occasionally, until soft but not brown.

2. Add the cumin and coriander and cook, stirring, for 2 minutes.

3. Add the courgettes, potato, stock and milk. Bring to the boil, cover and reduce the heat. Simmer gently for about 15 minutes until the vegetables are soft.

4. Leave to cool slightly, then tip into a food processor or blender and purée until smooth.

5. Season to taste with salt and pepper and reheat if necessary.

To microwave:
1. Put the butter, onion and garlic into a large casserole. Cover and cook on High for about 3 minutes or until soft, stirring once.

2. Add the cumin and coriander and cook on High for 1 minute.

3. Add the courgettes, potato and hot stock. Cover and cook on High for about 10 minutes, stirring once, or until the vegetables are soft.

4. Stir in the milk, then continue as steps 4 and 5.

To slow-cook:
1. Prepare as steps 1 and 2 and tip into the crockpot.

2. Add the courgettes, potatoes and hot stock and milk. Cover and cook on High for 2 hours or Low for 4–6 hours.

3. Continue as steps 4 and 5. Serve straight away.

To freeze:
Cool and freeze at the end of step 5.

Strawberry Soup with Whipped Cream

There is nothing quite so delicious as seasonal strawberries. They have a sweeter, more intense flavour than the hothouse varieties flown halfway round the world when they're not even ripe! This recipe is based on one created by the late Jane Grigson. In place of red wine, we've added the summery tipple, Pimm's No.1.

Serves 4–6

675g/1½lb ripe strawberries, hulled
1 tsp cornflour
about 5 tbsp orange juice
about 85g/3oz caster sugar
about 5 tbsp Pimm's No. 1
120ml/4fl oz double cream, whipped

1. Reserve 4–6 small whole strawberries for decoration. Blend the cornflour with the orange juice and set aside.

2. Thickly slice the remaining strawberries and put them into a large saucepan with the sugar and 1 tbsp water. Heat gently, stirring occasionally, until the sugar dissolves, the juice runs from the strawberries and the mixture begins to bubble. Simmer for 5 minutes. Stir in the cornflour and orange mixture, bring to the boil, then cook for 1 minute until slightly thickened and clear, stirring gently all the time.

3. Leave to cool slightly, then tip into a processor or blender and purée until smooth. Rub the mixture through a fine sieve. Leave to cool.

4. Stir in the Pimm's. Taste, adjusting the sweetness and adding more Pimms according to taste.

5. Serve chilled, floating a spoonful of whipped cream on top and decorating with the reserved strawberries.

To microwave:
1. As step 1.

2. Thickly slice the remaining strawberries and put them into a bowl with the sugar and 1 tbsp water. Cook on Medium-High for about 5 minutes, stirring occasionally, or until the sugar dissolves, the juice runs from the strawberries and the mixture begins to bubble. Stir in the cornflour and orange mixture, cover and cook on Medium-Low for about 10 minutes, stirring occasionally.

3. As steps 3–5.

Not suitable for slow-cooking.

To freeze:
Freeze at the end of step 3. To serve, thaw, then continue as steps 4 and 5.

Melon and Ginger Soup

Cantaloupe and galia melons are now grown in Britain so make
the most of them in this delicious, refreshing summer soup.
To check the melon is ripe, it should give slightly at the stalk
end and should smell fragrant.

Serves 4–6

115g/4oz caster sugar
1 ripe cantaloupe or galia melon
300ml/½ pint dry white wine
5cm/2in piece of fresh root ginger
150ml/¼ pint crème fraîche, plus extra to serve

1. Put the sugar in a large saucepan with 450ml/¾ pint water. Heat gently until the sugar has dissolved and the mixture comes to the boil. Leave to cool.

2. Halve and deseed the melon and scoop out all the flesh. Tip the melon (and any residual juice) into a food processor or blender and add the wine. Purée until smooth.

3. Transfer to a bowl and stir in the sugar syrup. Roughly grate the ginger and, gathering it up in your hand, squeeze hard so that the juice runs through your fingers and into the bowl (discard the pulp). Whisk in the crème fraîche.

4. Serve chilled, with a swirl of crème fraîche on the top of each bowl.

To microwave:
1. Put the sugar in a bowl with 450ml/¾ pint water. Cook on High, stirring occasionally, until the sugar dissolves and the mixture comes to the boil. Leave to cool.

2. As steps 2–4.

Not suitable for slow-cooking.

Not suitable for freezing.

Summer Fruit Soup

A refreshing and summery end to a meal. Use any summer fruits you like, such as strawberries, stoned cherries, peaches, and/or blueberries.

Serves 4–6

675g/1½lb summer fruits
3 tbsp lemon juice
2 tbsp caster sugar
150ml/¼ pint fruit juice, such as orange, pineapple or mango
300ml/½ pint sweet cider, plus extra if necessary
4 tbsp finely chopped fresh mint
mint leaves, for decoration

1. Put the fruit into a large saucepan with the lemon juice and sugar. Heat gently, stirring, until the sugar dissolves, the fruit juices run and the mixture begins to bubble.

2. Remove from the heat and stir in the fruit juice.

3. Tip into a food processor or blender and purée until smooth. Add the cider and purée again.

4. Rub the mixture through a fine sieve. Stir in the mint.

5. Serve chilled, decorated with a mint leaf or two.

To microwave:
1. Put the fruit into a bowl with the lemon juice and sugar. Cook on High, stirring occasionally, until the sugar dissolves, the fruit juices run and the mixture begins to bubble.

2. As steps 2–5.

Not suitable for slow-cooking.

To freeze:
Freeze at the end of step 4.

6 *Autumn Soups*

When the days get shorter and summer is over, there are still plenty of vegetables around, including the winter squashes, peppers, wild mushrooms, greens, the new season's celery and the wonderful autumn fruits. It's the hunting season for wild game, lamb is plentiful and there's lots of different fish and shellfish to enjoy.

Clear Vegetable Soup

You may think of peas and tomatoes as being summer crops but
their season stretches well into autumn when they can pair
beautifully with seasonal celery and leeks in this delicious soup. For
a more substantial affair, add some tiny dumplings with the
tomatoes and peas in step 2. Cover the soup while the dumplings
cook. For dumplings, see page 130.

Serves 4–6

1 litre/1¾ pints Vegetable Stock (see page 4)
2 carrots, diced
1 small leek, thinly sliced
2 small celery sticks, thinly sliced
350g/12oz tomatoes, skinned, deseeded, and chopped (see Cooks' tip on page 69)
115g/4oz fresh shelled or frozen peas
salt and freshly ground black pepper
2 tbsp chopped fresh parsley

1. Put the stock into a large saucepan and bring to the boil. Add the
carrots, leek and celery. Reduce the heat and simmer gently for
about 5 minutes or until the vegetables are just soft.

2. Stir in the tomatoes and peas and simmer gently for
2–3 minutes. Season to taste, stir in the parsley and serve.

To microwave:
1. Put half the hot stock into a large casserole and cook on High for about 5 minutes or until it just comes to the boil, stirring once. Stir in the carrots, leek and celery. Cover and cook on High for about 5 minutes, or until the vegetables are just soft, stirring once

2. Add the tomatoes and peas and cook on High for 2 minutes. Stir in the remaining hot stock and microwave a further 1 minute.

3. Season to taste, stir in the parsley and serve.

To slow-cook:
1. Put all the ingredients except the stock into the slow-cooker. Add the hot stock. Season lightly with salt.

2. Cover and cook on High for 2–3 hours or Low for 5–7 hours. Season to taste, stir in the parsley and serve.

To freeze:
Prepare to step 2 but don't add the parsley, then freeze. To serve, thaw and reheat thoroughly, then add the parsley.

Clear Chicken and Tomato Soup

A lightly flavoured soup which makes an ideal start to a meal. The egg whites help to keep the broth clear.

Serves 4

1 litre/1¾ pints Chicken Stock (see page 8)
1 onion, finely chopped
2 garlic cloves, halved
2 carrots, finely chopped
2 celery sticks, finely chopped
4 tomatoes, chopped
4 boneless chicken thighs, skin and fat removed
2 egg whites
salt and freshly ground black pepper
1 tbsp dry sherry (optional)

1. Put the stock in a large saucepan and add the onion, garlic, carrots, celery, tomatoes (including any juice) and chicken. Whisk the egg whites until frothy and add to the pan.

2. Heat gently, whisking continuously, until a thick frothy sludge starts to form on the surface. Stop whisking and continue heating until the mixture just comes to the boil. Immediately reduce the heat and simmer very gently for about 30 minutes.

3. Line a sieve with muslin and sit it over a large bowl. Carefully pour the mixture into the sieve, gently holding the top layer back and then finally allowing it to slide into the sieve.

4. Lift the chicken pieces from the sieve, rinse and dry on kitchen paper. Cut the chicken into small strips.

5. Pour the strained liquid into a clean pan and reheat gently until not quite boiling. Season to taste with salt and pepper and stir in the sherry, if using.

6. To serve, spoon the chicken pieces into warmed bowls and pour the soup over.

Not suitable for microwaving.

Not suitable for slow-cooking.

COOKS' TIP: Clearing the soup

During cooking, the vegetables and egg white will sit on the top, acting as a filter that will clarify the soup. If cooking is too quick, the surface will break, causing the soup to become cloudy.

Cullen Skink

This recipe is based on the smoked fish and potato soup traditionally served in Scotland. Shallots are in season this time of year and waxy salad potatoes are at their best in summer and autumn. Smoked haddock is available all year but haddock itself is really good in autumn so it's an ideal time to be enjoying it in any form. You can use larger waxy potatoes and dice them rather than slice if you prefer.

Serves 4

450g/1lb small, waxy potatoes, scrubbed and thinly sliced
450g/1lb smoked haddock fillet
2 shallots, finely chopped
600ml/1 pint Vegetable Stock (see page 4)
6 black peppercorns
300ml/½ pint milk
salt and freshly ground black pepper
chopped fresh parsley

1. Cook the potatoes in boiling salted water until tender.

2. Meanwhile, arrange the fish in a shallow pan and add the shallots, stock and peppercorns. Bring to the boil, reduce the heat and simmer very gently for about 10 minutes or until the fish is cooked.

3. Lift the fish from the pan, reserving the stock and shallots but discarding the peppercorns. Flake the fish, discarding the skin and bones.

4. Drain the potatoes and return them to the rinsed-out pan. Add the flaked fish and the reserved stock and shallots. Stir in the milk, then season to taste with salt and pepper.

5. Heat gently until hot. Serve sprinkled with parsley.

To microwave:
1. Arrange the fish in a shallow dish. Add three-quarters of the hot stock, the shallots and peppercorns. Cover and cook on High for 5 minutes. Cover and leave to stand.

2. Meanwhile, put the potatoes into a large casserole with the remaining stock. Cover and cook on High for 8–10 minutes, stirring once or twice, until tender.

3. As step 3.

4. Add the fish to the potatoes in the casserole. Stir in the reserved stock and shallots. Add the milk and season to taste.

5. As step 5.

Not suitable for slow-cooking.

Not suitable for freezing.

Creamy Onion and Rosemary Soup

Home-grown onions are at their best in summer and autumn but this is more of a chilly day soup than a winter cooler so we've put it in this section. If you don't have rosemary to hand, try sage or thyme instead for a different, but equally delicious, soup.

Serves 4

25g/1oz butter
450g/1lb onions, thinly sliced
1 large garlic clove, thinly sliced
1 tbsp fresh chopped or 1 tsp dried rosemary
750ml/1¼ pints Vegetable Stock (see page 4)
salt and freshly ground black pepper
150ml/¼ pint double cream
4 tbsp dry sherry (optional)
snipped fresh chives, to garnish

1. Melt the butter in a large saucepan and stir in the onions, garlic and rosemary. Cover and cook very gently for about 10 minutes, stirring occasionally, until soft but not brown.

2. Stir in the stock, bring to the boil and reduce the heat. Simmer gently for about 15 minutes, until the onions are very soft.

3. Leave to cool slightly, then tip the mixture into a food processor or blender and purée until smooth. Rub through a sieve to remove any woody pieces of rosemary.

4. Season to taste with salt and pepper, then stir in the cream and sherry, if using. Reheat gently and serve garnished with chives.

To microwave:
1. Put the butter, onions, garlic and rosemary into a large casserole. Cover and cook on High for about 5 minutes, stirring once, or until the onions are very soft.

2. Stir in the stock, cover and cook on High for 10 minutes, stirring once or twice.

3. As steps 3 and 4.

To slow-cook:
1. Prepare as steps 1 and 2 and tip into the crockpot.

2. Add the hot stock.

3. Cover and cook on High for 2 hours or Low for 4–6 hours.

4. Continue as step 3. Tip back into the crock pot and stir in the cream and sherry, if using. Leave on Low until ready to serve, garnished with chives.

To freeze:
Cool and freeze at the end of step 3. Reheat the soup and, just before serving, add the cream and sherry, if using. Garnish with chives.

Two-tomato Soup

Outdoor tomatoes ripen later than their hothouse counterparts and they are ideal for this well-flavoured soup. It's comforting when the warmth of summer is leaving us and you want something tempting for a simple lunch or supper with some crusty bread, cheese and pickles or chutney made, perhaps, with some of your own produce.

For the best flavour, use a combination of fresh and canned tomatoes. There's no need to skin the fresh tomatoes in this recipe. Don't be put off by the generous amount of sugar, which is needed to season the soup – it's allowed once in a while!

Serves 4–6

15g/½oz butter
1 tbsp olive oil
1 large garlic clove, crushed or finely chopped
1 onion, finely chopped
450g/1lb ripe tomatoes, quartered
400g/14oz can chopped tomatoes
2 tbsp tomato purée
1 tbsp caster sugar
600ml/1 pint Chicken Stock (see page 8) or Vegetable Stock (see page 4)
1 tbsp chopped fresh herbs, such as thyme, oregano, basil and parsley
up to 600ml/1 pint milk
salt and freshly ground black pepper

1. Put the butter, oil, garlic and onion into a large saucepan. Cook gently for about 5 minutes, stirring occasionally, until soft but not brown.

2. Add the fresh and canned tomatoes, tomato purée, sugar, stock and herbs. Bring to the boil, cover, reduce the heat and simmer gently for about 20 minutes.

3. Leave to cool slightly, then tip the mixture into a food processor or blender and purée until smooth. Rub through a sieve to remove seeds and skins.

4. Return the puréed soup to the pan. Add the milk and season to taste with salt and pepper.

5. Reheat and serve.

To microwave:
1. Put the butter, oil, garlic and onion into a large casserole. Cover and cook on High for about 3 minutes until soft, stirring once.

2. Add the fresh and canned tomatoes, tomato purée, sugar, half the hot stock and the herbs. Cover and cook on High for about 15 minutes, stirring once or twice.

3. Add the remaining stock, then continue as steps 3–5.

To slow-cook:
1. Prepare as steps 1 and 2. Bring to the boil and tip into the crock pot.

2. Cover and cook on High for 2 hours or Low for 4–6 hours.

3. Continue as step 3.

4. At step 4 tip back into the slow-cooker and leave on Low until ready to serve.

To freeze:
Cool and freeze at the end of step 4.

Mushroom and Herb Soup

This soup is a favourite with children and adults alike. For a dark, well-flavoured soup, use flat, open mushrooms; for a light, delicate soup, use button or closed-cup mushrooms. It is a classic autumn soup if you can find wild field mushrooms, but, of course, you can use cultivated ones at any time of year. If you are using wild mushrooms, be absolutely certain you have identified them correctly. If in doubt, stick to the cultivated variety.

Serves 4–6

40g/1½oz butter
2 onions, finely chopped
225g/8oz mushrooms, thinly sliced
25g/1oz plain flour
900ml/1½ pints Vegetable Stock (see page 4) or Chicken Stock (see page 8)
300ml/½ pint milk
2 tbsp chopped fresh parsley, plus extra for garnish
1 tbsp fresh thyme leaves
salt and freshly ground black pepper
1 tbsp lemon juice
3 tbsp double cream (optional)

1. Melt the butter in a large saucepan and add the onions. Cook gently for about 5 minutes, stirring occasionally, until soft but not brown.

2. Stir in the mushrooms, then the flour. Gradually stir in the stock. Add the milk and herbs. Bring to the boil, stirring. Cover, reduce the heat and simmer gently for 10 minutes.

3. Leave to cool slightly, then tip the mixture into a food processor or blender and purée until smooth. Season to taste with salt and pepper.

4. Stir in the lemon juice and cream. Serve garnished with extra chopped parsley.

To microwave:
1. Put the butter and onions in a large casserole. Cover and cook on High for about 5 minutes, stirring once, until soft.

2. Stir in the mushrooms, then the flour. Gradually stir in half the hot stock and the herbs. Cover and cook on High for 10 minutes, stirring once or twice. Add the remaining stock and the milk.

3. As steps 3 and 4.

Not suitable for slow-cooking.

To freeze:
Cool and freeze at the end of step 3. To serve, thaw and reheat the soup, then continue with step 4.

Fennel and Apple Soup

Fennel, with its delicate aniseed flavour, is in season from the height of summer through autumn and blends beautifully with sweet autumn-picked apples. This soup is delicious served hot or chilled. If you want a really smooth finish, rub it through a fine sieve at the end of step 3.

Serves 4–6

2 fennel bulbs
25g/1oz butter
1 onion, finely chopped
3 eating apples, peeled, cored and chopped
1 litre/1¾ pints Vegetable Stock (see page 4) or Chicken Stock (see page 8)
salt and freshly ground black pepper
soured cream or thick Greek-style plain yogurt

1. Trim and thinly slice the fennel, reserving a few of the green fronds for garnish.

2. Melt the butter in a large saucepan and add the onion. Cook gently for about 5 minutes, stirring occasionally, until soft but not brown. Stir in the fennel and apples and cook, stirring, for 1–2 minutes.

3. Add the stock, bring to the boil and reduce the heat. Simmer gently for 20–30 minutes until the fennel is very soft.

4. Leave to cool slightly, then tip into a food processor or blender and purée until smooth. Season to taste with salt and pepper.

5. Ladle into bowls and serve topped with a spoonful of soured cream or yogurt. Snip the reserved fennel fronds on top.

To microwave:
1. As step 1.

2. Put the butter and onion into a large casserole, cover and cook for 2 minutes. Stir in the fennel and apples, cover and cook for 3 minutes, stirring once.

3. Add half the hot stock. Cover and cook on High for about 15 minutes, stirring once, or until the fennel is very soft.

4. Add the remaining stock and continue with step 4.

5. As step 5.

To slow-cook:
1. Prepare as steps 1 and 2 and tip into the crockpot.

2. Add the hot stock, cover and cook on High for 2 hours or Low for 4–6 hours.

3. As steps 4 and 5.

To freeze:
Cool and freeze at the end of step 4. To serve, thaw, then reheat and garnish as step 5.

Minestrone

This particular version of the classic Italian soup was originally developed as a quick microwave soup, but it works just as well on the hob. It uses a whole variety of autumn vegetables and is perfect for a light lunch or supper with some warm ciabatta bread. If you like, make it even more substantial by adding a drained can of haricot beans. It's also good with a finely chopped bacon rasher added with the vegetables in step 1.

Serves 4

1 tbsp olive oil
1 small onion, finely chopped
1 large garlic clove, thinly sliced
2 carrots, diced
2 small celery sticks, thinly sliced
1 turnip, diced
900ml/1½ pints Vegetable Stock (see page 4)
3 sun-dried tomatoes, finely chopped
50g/1¾oz fresh shelled or frozen peas
50g/1¾oz small dried pasta shapes
50g/1¾oz cavolo nero, kale or green cabbage, finely shredded
2 tbsp chopped fresh parsley
salt and freshly ground black pepper

To serve:
freshly grated or shaved Parmesan cheese

1. Put the oil, onion, garlic, carrots, celery and turnip into a large saucepan. Cook gently for about 5 minutes, stirring occasionally, until slightly soft but not brown.

2. Add the stock and bring to the boil. Cover, reduce the heat and simmer gently for about 10 minutes.

3. Stir in the tomatoes, peas and pasta. Simmer gently for 8–10 minutes, stirring once or twice, until the pasta is just tender.

4. Stir in the cavolo nero and parsley. Simmer for 2–3 minutes, then remove from the heat and leave to stand for 2–3 minutes. Season to taste with salt and pepper.

5. Serve sprinkled with Parmesan cheese.

To microwave:
1. Put the oil, onion, garlic, carrots, celery and turnip into a large casserole. Stir in half the hot stock. Cover and cook on High for about 5 minutes, stirring once or twice, until the vegetables are just tender.

2. Stir in the tomatoes, peas, pasta and remaining stock. Cook on High for about 5 minutes, stirring occasionally, or until the soup comes to the boil.

3. Stir in the cabbage and parsley. Cook on High for 2–3 minutes. Season to taste with salt and pepper.

4. As step 5.

To slow-cook:
1. Prepare as step 1 and tip into the crockpot.

2. Add the hot stock, cover and cook on High for 2 hours or Low for 4 hours.

3. Add the pasta, cavolo nero, tomatoes, peas and parsley, re-cover and cook on High for a further 1 hour. Season to taste with salt and pepper.

4. As step 4.

Not suitable for freezing.

Butternut Squash, Cumin and Coriander Soup

Butternut squash has brilliant orange, sweet flesh and has become a very popular autumn/winter vegetable. It gives this soup its beautiful colour. You can substitute any other winter squash, pumpkin being an excellent alternative. You can also serve it with croûtons (see page 16).

Serves 4

550g/1¼lb butternut squash
40g/1½oz butter
1 onion, thinly sliced
1 tsp ground cumin
225g/8oz potatoes, peeled and thinly sliced
750ml/1¼ pints Chicken Stock (see page 8) or Vegetable Stock (see page 4)
150ml/¼ pint double cream
salt and freshly ground black pepper
4 tbsp chopped fresh coriander

1. Cut the squash into quarters and scoop out and discard the seeds. Peel and slice the flesh.

2. Melt the butter in a large saucepan and add the onion. Cook gently for about 5 minutes, stirring occasionally, until soft but not brown.

3. Stir in the cumin, squash and potatoes and cook, stirring, for 2–3 minutes. Add the stock. Bring to the boil, cover, reduce the heat and simmer gently for about 20 minutes or until the squash is very soft.

4. Leave to cool slightly, then tip into a food processor or blender and purée until smooth. Add the cream and purée again. Season to taste with salt and pepper.

5. Reheat gently, stir in the coriander and serve.

To microwave:
1. As step 1.

2. Put the butter and onion into a large casserole. Cover and cook on High for 3 minutes or until soft, stirring once.

3. Stir in the cumin, squash, potato and half the hot stock. Cover and cook on High for about 15 minutes, stirring once or twice, or until the vegetables are very soft.

4. Add the remaining stock, then continue as step 4.

5. As step 5.

To slow-cook:
1. Prepare as step 1 and tip into the crockpot.

2. Add the hot stock and remaining ingredients.

3. Cover and cook on High for 2–3 hours or Low for 5–7 hours.

4. As step 5.

To freeze:
Cool and freeze at the end of step 4. Reheat and garnish as step 5.

114

Fennel and Bean Soup

Fennel is in season from late summer to mid autumn and has a wonderful aniseed flavour, while the beans add substance to the soup. It goes beautifully with creamy cannellini or haricot beans.

Serves 4–6

2 tbsp olive oil
1 onion, finely chopped
1 leek, thinly sliced
2 large garlic cloves, crushed
1 large fennel bulb, quartered lengthways and thinly sliced
900ml/1½ pints Chicken Stock (see page 8) or Vegetable Stock (see page 4)
400g/14oz can cannellini or haricot beans, drained
300ml/½ pint milk
salt and freshly ground black pepper

To serve:
freshly shaved Parmesan cheese,
snipped fresh chives and lemon wedges

1. Put the oil, onion, leek, garlic and fennel into a large saucepan. Cook gently for 10–15 minutes, stirring occasionally, or until the vegetables have softened and are just beginning to colour.

2. Add the stock and beans. Bring to the boil, cover and reduce the heat. Simmer gently for about 15 minutes or until the vegetables are very soft.

3. Either leave the soup chunky or leave to cool slightly, then tip about two-thirds of the mixture into a food processor or blender and purée until smooth. Return the purée to the mixture remaining in the pan.

4. Stir in the milk and season to taste with salt and pepper.

5. Reheat and serve topped with Parmesan shavings and chives. Let each person squeeze a lemon wedge over their serving, adding juice to taste.

To microwave:
1. Put the oil, onion, leek, garlic and fennel into a large casserole. Cover and cook on High for about 7 minutes, stirring occasionally, or until the vegetables are very soft.

2. Add half the hot stock and the beans. Cover and cook on High for about 5 minutes, then on Medium for about 10 minutes, stirring once.

3. Add the remaining stock and continue as steps 3–5.

To slow-cook:
1. Prepare as step 1 and tip into the crockpot.

2. Add the hot stock and remaining ingredients.

3. Cover and cook on High for 2–3 hours or Low for 5–7 hours.

4. Continue as step 5.

To freeze:
Cool and freeze at the end of step 4. Thaw and reheat to serve.

Sweetcorn and Tuna Chowder

Sweetcorn and tuna are ever-popular bedfellows. Here we've used fresh corn kernels. To cut them off the cobs see page 86. You can, of course, use frozen or canned instead.

Serves 4

40g/1½oz butter
1 onion, thinly sliced
1 carrot, finely chopped
2 celery sticks, thinly sliced
3 tbsp plain flour
600ml/1 pint milk
600ml/1 pint hot Vegetable Stock (see page 4)
1 red pepper, deseeded and chopped
225g/8oz fresh sweetcorn kernels from 3 smallish cobs
finely grated zest and juice of 1 lemon
200g/7oz can tuna in brine, drained and flaked
salt and freshly ground black pepper
100g/3½oz mature Cheddar cheese, grated

1. Melt the butter in a large saucepan and stir in the onion, carrot and celery. Cook gently for about 10 minutes, stirring occasionally, or until soft but not brown.

2. Stir in the flour and cook for 1–2 minutes. Gradually stir in the milk, then cook, stirring continuously, until the mixture boils and thickens.

3. Stir in the stock, pepper and sweetcorn. Cover and simmer gently for 10–15 minutes until the vegetables are tender.

4. Add the lemon zest and juice and the drained tuna. Season to taste with salt and pepper.

5. Reheat gently and serve, topping each bowl of soup with a sprinkling of cheese.

To microwave:
1. Put the butter, onion, carrot and celery into a large casserole. Cover and cook on High for about 5 minutes, stirring once or twice, until soft.

2. Stir in the flour, then gradually stir in the milk. Cook on High for about 5 minutes, stirring occasionally, or until the mixture comes to the boil and thickens.

3. Stir in the stock, pepper and sweetcorn. Cover and cook on High for about 10 minutes, stirring once, or until the vegetables are tender.

4. Continue as steps 4 and 5.

To slow-cook:
1. Prepare as step 1 and tip into the crockpot.

2. Add the hot stock and remaining ingredients.

3. Cover and cook on High for 2–3 hours or Low for 5–7 hours.

4. Continue as step 5.

Not suitable for freezing.

Haricot Bean Soup with Pasta, Parsley and Parmesan

Red peppers are in season in summer and autumn. Shallots come into their own now, too. These, combined with carrots and creamy haricot beans, make a delicious, chunky soup, made more substantial with the addition of pasta and enriched with Parmesan cheese. Serve it with a selection of warmed Italian-style breads.

Serves 4

1 tbsp olive oil
1 shallot, finely chopped
1 large garlic clove, crushed
1 small red pepper, deseeded and diced
1 carrot, diced
1.2 litres/2 pints Vegetable Stock (see page 4)
400g/14oz can haricot beans, drained and rinsed
25g/1oz small dried pasta shapes
salt and freshly ground black pepper
4 tbsp finely chopped fresh parsley
4 tbsp freshly grated Parmesan cheese

1. Put the oil, shallot and garlic into a large saucepan. Cook gently for about 5 minutes, stirring occasionally, until soft but not brown.

2. Add the pepper, carrot and stock. Bring to the boil, cover and reduce the heat. Simmer gently for 15–20 minutes.

3. Add the beans and pasta. Cover and cook gently for 8–10 minutes, or until the pasta and vegetables are tender.

4. Season to taste with salt and pepper and stir in the parsley. Serve piping hot, topped with the Parmesan cheese.

To microwave:
1. Put the oil, shallot and garlic into a large casserole. Cover and cook on High for 3 minutes until soft, stirring once.

2. Add the pepper, carrot and half the hot stock. Cover and cook on High for 10 minutes, stirring once.

3. Add the beans and pasta. Cover and cook on High for about 8 minutes, or until the pasta and vegetables are tender, stirring once or twice.

4. Stir in the remaining stock and continue as step 4.

To slow-cook:
1. Prepare as step 1 and tip into the crockpot.

2. Add the pepper, carrot and hot stock. Cover and cook on High for 2 hours or Low for 4–6 hours.

3. Continue as step 3. Cover and cook on High a further 1 hour.

4. As step 4.

Not suitable for freezing.

Pasta Soup with Mediterranean Herbs

Tomatoes are still in season well into autumn and make a fresh-tasting soup combined with lots of wonderful fragrant herbs and pasta – a classic combination. It is good served with freshly shaved Parmesan cheese and Hot Garlic Bread (see page 18) or Bruschetta (see page 19). To skin tomatoes, see page 69.

Serves 4–6

2 tbsp olive oil
1 onion, finely chopped
2 large garlic cloves, finely chopped
2 lean streaky bacon rashers, finely chopped
1.2 litres/2 pints Chicken Stock (see page 8)
175g/6oz small dried pasta shapes, such as conchiglie
1 tbsp chopped fresh thyme leaves
1 tbsp chopped fresh oregano
salt and freshly ground black pepper
4 ripe tomatoes, skinned, deseeded and chopped
about 10 fresh basil leaves

1. Heat the oil in a large saucepan and add the onion, garlic and bacon. Cook gently for about 10 minutes, stirring occasionally, until soft and beginning to brown.

2. Add the stock and bring to the boil.

3. Stir in the pasta, thyme and oregano and season with salt and pepper. Bring back to the boil, reduce the heat and simmer gently for about 10 minutes until the pasta is soft.

4. Adjust the seasoning to taste and stir in the tomatoes. Tear the basil into shreds, add to the soup and serve.

To microwave:
1. Put the oil, onion, garlic and bacon into a large casserole. Cook on High for about 5 minutes, stirring once, until soft.

2. Add the hot stock and cook on High for about 5 minutes or until the mixture comes to the boil, stirring once.

3. Stir in the pasta, thyme, oregano, salt and pepper. Cook, uncovered, on High for about 10 minutes, stirring once or twice, or until the pasta is soft.

4. As step 4.

To slow-cook:
1. Prepare as step 1 and tip into the crockpot.

2. Add the hot stock and remaining ingredients.

3. Cover and cook on High for 1 hour or Low for 3 hours.

4. As step 4.

Not suitable for freezing.

Chinese Chicken and Vegetable Soup

Chinese leaves are at their best in autumn and are perfect thickly
shredded in this quick-to-make soup, which is just as good made
with thinly sliced pork fillet in place of chicken. Peppers are still
plentiful at this time of year but home-grown baby sweetcorn has a
very short season so enjoy this now at its best.

Serves 4–6

1 tbsp sunflower oil
1 skinless chicken breast, thinly sliced
2 large garlic cloves, crushed
1 small head of Chinese leaves, quartered lengthways and thickly sliced
85g/3oz mushrooms, such as oyster or shiitake
1 small red pepper, deseeded and diced
55g/2oz baby sweetcorn, thinly sliced
1 litre/1¾ pints Chicken Stock (see page 8)
3 tbsp soy sauce
85g/3oz dried thread noodles
5cm/2in piece of fresh root ginger
4 spring onions, thinly sliced
salt and freshly ground black pepper
2 tbsp chopped fresh coriander or parsley

1. Heat the oil in a large saucepan or wok. Add the chicken and
cook quickly, stirring, until cooked through and golden brown.

2. Stir in the garlic and cook, stirring, for 1 minute. Add the
Chinese leaves, mushrooms, pepper and sweetcorn. Cook for
1–2 minutes, stirring.

3. Add the stock and soy sauce. Break the noodles into the pan.

4. Roughly grate the ginger and, scooping it up in your hand,
squeeze hard so that the juice runs through your fingers and into
the pan (discard the pulp).

5. Add the spring onions, bring to the boil, reduce the heat and simmer gently for 3–5 minutes until the noodles are soft.

6. Season to taste with salt and pepper and stir in the coriander or parsley.

To microwave:
1. Put the oil into a large casserole and stir in the chicken and garlic. Cover and cook on High for about 3 minutes, stirring once, or until the chicken is cooked through.

2. Add the Chinese leaves, mushrooms, pepper and sweetcorn. Cover and cook for 2 minutes.

3. Add the hot stock and soy sauce. Break the noodles into the casserole and stir well.

4. As step 4.

5. Add the spring onions, cover and cook on High for about 8 minutes, or until the mixture has come to the boil and the noodles are soft, stirring once or twice.

6. As step 6.

Not suitable for slow-cooking.

Not suitable for freezing.

COOKS' TIP: Ginger
If, like me, you tend to lose pieces of fresh ginger root at the back of the fridge, only to shrivel up before they are used, keep a bottle of root ginger sauce handy instead. It makes an excellent alternative to ginger juice.

Pheasant and Field Mushroom Soup

In the UK, the pheasant season runs from 1 October to 1 February.
This is the ideal way to make a small pheasant go round for four
people. If you can't get hold of large field mushrooms, use
cultivated flat portobello ones instead.

Serves 4

1 tbsp olive oil

1 small hen pheasant, quartered

1 small onion, chopped

1 litre/1¾ pints Chicken or Game Stock (see page 8)

1 tbsp fresh thyme leaves

1 bay leaf

salt and freshly ground black pepper

1 potato, peeled and diced

1 carrot, diced

1 kohlrabi or large turnip, diced

2 large flat field mushrooms, peeled, halved and sliced

1 tbsp redcurrant jelly

2 tbsp plain flour

4 tbsp water

4 tbsp port

1 tsp soy sauce

a little chopped fresh parsley, to garnish

1. Heat the oil in a large saucepan and brown the pheasant portions on
all sides. Add the onion, stock, thyme, bay leaf and a little seasoning.
Bring to the boil, reduce the heat, cover and simmer for 1 hour.

2. Discard the bay leaf and lift out the pheasant. Set aside to cool a little.

3. Put the potato, carrot, kohlrabi or turnip, mushrooms and
redcurrant jelly in the stock in the pan. Bring back to the boil,
reduce the heat, partially cover and simmer for 20 minutes.

4. When the pheasant is cool enough to handle, cut all the meat off the bones, discarding the skin. Chop and reserve the meat.

5. When the vegetables are tender, blend the flour with the water and port; stir into the soup. Bring to the boil, stirring, and simmer for 2 minutes. Add the chopped pheasant and heat through. Add the soy sauce and re-season to taste with salt and pepper. Ladle into warm soup bowls and garnish with a little chopped parsley.

To microwave:
1. Brown the pheasant as step 1 and then place in a casserole and continue as step 1, using hot stock. Cover and microwave on High for 10 minutes until boiling, then cook on Medium for 40 minutes or until the pheasant is tender, rearranging the portions once or twice.

2. As step 2.

3. Continue as step 3, cover and microwave on High for 10 minutes, stirring once or twice.

4. Continue as steps 4 and 5 but cook on High for 2 minutes, stirring once to thicken the soup when the flour is added.

To slow-cook:
1. Brown the pheasant as step 1.

2. Put all the other ingredients including the hot stock in the slow-cooker. Blend the flour with the water and port and stir in with the soy sauce. Add the pheasant. Cover and cook on High for 3–4 hours or Low for 6–8 hours, or until the pheasant is meltingly tender.

3. Discard the bay leaf. Lift the pheasant out of the slow-cooker. When cool enough to handle, take all the meat off the bones,

discarding the skin. Chop the meat and return to the slow-cooker. Add the soy sauce, taste and re-season if necessary.

4. Ladle into warm soup bowls and garnish with a little chopped parsley.

To freeze:
Cool, then freeze before adding the soy sauce. To serve, thaw, reheat and season with soy sauce and more salt and pepper as necessary. Garnish as step 5.

Chocolate and Vanilla Soup

This one is for chocolate lovers! Similar to a chocolate fondue, this dessert soup is at its most indulgent when you use a chocolate containing at least 50 per cent cocoa solids, preferably 70 per cent. It's best served at room temperature. We've chosen autumnal fruits but you could serve in summer with stoned cherries, blueberries, peaches and strawberries instead.

Serves 4–6

300ml/½ pint milk
1 vanilla pod
225g/8oz plain dark chocolate

To serve:
mixture of fresh fruits, such as raspberries, blackberries, pears, and plums,
stoned and cut into bite-size pieces, if necessary
crisp biscuits, such as amaretti

1. Pour the milk into a non-stick pan. Split the vanilla pod and scrape out the seeds. Add the pod and seeds to the milk. Place the pan on a low heat and slowly bring the milk just to the boil. Remove from the heat and leave to stand for 5 minutes.

2. Meanwhile, break the chocolate into a bowl and place over a pan of simmering water, stirring occasionally, until melted.

3. Remove the vanilla pod from the milk and rinse and dry it to use again. Pour the flavoured milk over the chocolate and gently whisk until smooth. Leave to cool to room temperature.

4. Warm some individual serving bowls. Spoon some fruit pieces into each bowl and pour the chocolate soup over the top. Serve with crisp biscuits.

To microwave:
1. Pour the milk into a bowl. Split the vanilla pod and scrape out the seeds. Add the pod and seeds to the milk. Heat the milk on Medium-Low for about 3 minutes or until the mixture comes just to the boil. Leave to stand for 5 minutes.

2. Meanwhile, break the chocolate into a bowl and heat on Medium-Low for about 10 minutes, stirring occasionally, until melted.

3. As steps 3 and 4.

Not suitable for slow-cooking.

Not suitable for freezing.

7 Winter Soups

When the nights draw in and the days are colder, there is nothing so comforting as a hearty bowl of rib-sticking soup. These recipes feature all the lovely seasonal roots and tubers, some legumes, pasta or rice to pad them out, and rich meats and poultry to add depth of flavour and goodness. Most make a meal in themselves but some are elegant enough to start a celebration dinner.

Cock-a-leekie with Mini Dumplings

Make the most of winter leeks in this classic soup. For a lighter version
to serve as a first course (in which case the recipe will serve 6), omit
the dumplings and simply garnish with chopped fresh parsley.

Serves 4

450g/1lb leeks
25g/1oz butter
1 large chicken leg portion
1 litre/1¼ pints Chicken Stock (see page 8)
1 bouquet garni (see Cooks' tip on page 7)
salt and freshly ground black pepper
8 ready-to-eat dried prunes, each cut into 4 slivers

For the dumplings:
100g/3½oz self-raising flour
a pinch of salt
freshly ground black pepper
50g/1¾oz shredded suet
2 tbsp chopped fresh parsley

1. Thinly slice the white parts of the leeks, reserving the green
parts.

2. Melt the butter in a large saucepan and brown the chicken on all
sides. Add the white leeks and cook gently for about 5 minutes,
stirring occasionally, until soft.

3. Add the stock and bouquet garni. Season with salt and pepper.
Bring to the boil, then simmer gently for about 30 minutes or until
the chicken is very tender.

4. Lift out the chicken and cut the meat into small pieces, discarding
the skin and bones.

5. Make the dumplings. Sift the flour with salt and some pepper. Stir in the suet. Add sufficient cold water to make a soft but manageable dough. With floured fingers, shape the dough into about 16 small balls.

6. Thinly slice the reserved green leeks and add to the casserole with the prunes and chicken. Bring to the boil.

7. Drop the dumplings into the soup, cover and simmer gently for about 15 minutes, or until swollen and cooked.

To microwave (without the dumplings):
1. As step 1.

2. Put the butter and white leeks into a large casserole. Cover and cook on High for about 3 minutes until soft, stirring once.

3. Add the chicken, half the hot stock and the bouquet garni. Season with salt and pepper. Cover and cook on High for about 5 minutes or until the mixture comes to the boil, stirring once. Continue cooking on Medium for about 15 minutes or until the chicken is very tender, stirring once or twice.

4. As step 4 above.

To slow-cook (without the dumplings):
1. Prepare as steps 1 and 2, then tip into the crockpot.

2. Add the hot stock, bouquet garni and seasoning.

3. Cover and cook on High for 2–3 hours or Low for 5–7 hours.

4. Continue as steps 4 and 6 (omit step 5). Add to the crockpot and cook on High for a further 1 hour or Low a further 2 hours.

To freeze:
Omit the dumplings, cool and freeze at the end of step 6.

Creamy Brussels Sprout Soup with Smoked Lardons

Sprouts are the classic winter vegetable, and in this recipe there is no need to trim them as you would if preparing to boil or steam them. Simply trim the bases. Smoked lardons can be bought ready prepared in supermarkets. Look for those prepared from outdoor-reared, preferably free-range pigs.

Serves 4–6

15g/½oz butter
1 onion, chopped
750ml/1¼ pints Chicken Stock (see page 8) or Vegetable Stock (see page 4)
450g/1lb Brussels sprouts, trimmed
1 potato, peeled and diced
a good grating of fresh nutmeg
salt and freshly ground black pepper
75g/2½oz smoked lardons
2 tbsp plain flour
4 tbsp milk
6 tbsp double cream

1. Melt the butter in a large saucepan. Add the onion and fry gently, stirring, for 2 minutes until softened but not browned.

2. Add the stock, sprouts, potato and nutmeg. Season with salt and pepper.

3. Bring to the boil, reduce the heat and partially cover. Simmer for 20 minutes or until the sprouts and potato are really tender.

4. Meanwhile, dry-fry the lardons in a small frying pan until crisp and golden. Drain on kitchen paper.

5. Purée the soup in a blender or food processor. Return to the pan. Blend the flour with the milk and stir in with 4 tbsp of the cream. Bring to the boil and cook for 2 minutes, stirring, until thickened. Season to taste with salt and pepper.

6. Ladle the soup into bowls and garnish with a swirl of the remaining cream and the crispy lardons.

To microwave:
1. Put the butter and onion into a large casserole. Cover and cook on High for 2 minutes until soft, stirring once.

2. Stir in the sprouts, potato, nutmeg and seasoning to the hot stock. Cook on High for about 5 minutes, stirring occasionally, until the mixture comes to the boil.

3. Cover and cook on Medium for about 15 minutes or until the sprouts and potatoes are tender, stirring once or twice.

4. As steps 4–6.

To slow-cook:
1. Melt the butter in a frying pan and cook the onion gently for 2 minutes, until softened but not browned. Stir in the flour, then blend in the stock. Bring to the boil and pour into the crockpot.

2. Add the sprouts, potato, nutmeg, salt and pepper.

3. Cover and cook on High for 2 hours or Low for 4–6 hours.

4. Meanwhile, cook the lardons as step 4.

5. Purée the soup as step 5, taste and re-season. If necessary, tip back in the slow-cooker to keep warm until ready to serve or ladle into bowls and garnish with the lardons.

To freeze:
Cool, then freeze after puréeing at step 5 (but don't cook the lardons at step 4 until ready to serve). Don't thicken or add the cream until reheating when ready to serve.

French Onion Soup

Onions are available all year but are a really useful winter crop, delicious on their own or paired with the wonderful roots, greens and tubers of the season. This soup traditionally has slices of cheese-topped French bread floating on the top. To lighten it up, you could serve it instead with some tiny Parmesan Croûtons (see page 17).

Serves 4

25g/1oz butter
450g/1lb onions, thinly sliced in rings
1 tsp caster sugar
2 tbsp cornflour
1 litre/1¾ pints Beef Stock (see page 6)
salt and freshly ground black pepper

To serve:
4 French bread slices
50g/1¾oz Gruyère or Cheddar cheese, grated

1. Melt the butter in a large saucepan. Add the onions and sugar and cook gently for about 15 minutes, stirring occasionally, until very soft and light golden brown.

2. Stir in the cornflour, then gradually stir in the stock. Season with salt and pepper.

3. Bring to the boil, stirring continuously, until the soup thickens slightly. Cover, reduce the heat and simmer gently for about 30 minutes.

4. Top the bread slices with cheese and grill until bubbling and golden. Float one slice on top of each serving of soup. Alternatively, ladle the soup into flameproof dishes, float the cheese-topped bread on top and put under a hot grill until bubbling and golden.

To microwave:
1. Put the butter, onions and sugar into a large casserole. Cover and cook on High for about 5 minutes, stirring once, until soft.

2. Stir in the cornflour, then gradually stir in the hot stock. Season with salt and pepper.

3. Cook on High for about 5 minutes, stirring occasionally, or until the soup comes to the boil and thickens slightly. Cover and cook on Medium for about 15 minutes, stirring once or twice.

4. As step 4.

To slow-cook:
1. Put the butter in the slow-cooker on High and leave for about 15 minutes to melt. Add the onions and sugar and toss well. Cover and cook on High for 2–3 hours until soft and turning golden.

2. Stir in the cornflour, then add the hot stock. Season with salt and pepper.

3. Cook on High for a further 1–2 hours. Season to taste with salt and pepper.

4. As step 4.

To freeze:
Cool and freeze at the end of step 3. Reheat and continue with step 4.

COOKS' TIP: Spicing It Up
Try adding a good dash of Worcestershire sauce or brandy with the stock in step 2.

Shallot and Spinach Soup

Shallots are in season in autumn through winter. They impart a sweet, mild onion flavour, which goes beautifully with year-round spinach. The addition of potato naturally thickens the mixture when puréed.

Serves 4–6

25g/1oz butter
225g/8oz shallots, chopped
1 potato, peeled and thinly sliced
900ml/1½ pints Chicken Stock (see page 8) or Vegetable Stock (see page 4)
salt and freshly ground black pepper
225g/8oz fresh spinach, shredded, if large
a good pinch of freshly grated nutmeg
2 tbsp double cream

1. Melt the butter in a large saucepan. Add the shallots and cook gently for about 5 minutes, stirring occasionally, until soft but not brown.

2. Stir in the potato, stock and salt and pepper. Bring to the boil, cover and simmer gently for about 15 minutes until the potato is very soft.

3. Add the spinach and nutmeg. Bring to the boil, reduce the heat and simmer gently for 5 minutes.

4. Leave to cool slightly, then tip into a food processor or blender and purée until smooth.

5. Reheat, adjusting the seasoning if necessary. Stir in the cream and serve.

To microwave:
1. Put the butter and shallots into a large casserole. Cover and cook on High for about 3 minutes, or until soft.

2. Stir in the potato, half the hot stock and the salt and pepper. Cook on High for about 10 minutes, stirring once or twice, or until the potato is very soft.

3. Add the spinach and nutmeg. Cover and cook on high for 5 minutes, stirring once.

4. Stir in the remaining stock and continue as steps 4–5.

To slow-cook:
1. Fry the shallots in the butter in a frying pan for 2–3 minutes to soften. Tip into the crockpot.

2. Add all the remaining ingredients except the cream. Cover and cook on High for 2–3 hours or Low for 5–7 hours.

3. As steps 4 and 5.

To freeze:
Cool and freeze at the end of step 4. To serve, thaw, then continue as step 5.

Spiced Parsnip and Potato Soup

Parsnips are best when they've been touched by the frosts so
are a great winter crop. Their sweetness is complemented by
spices, so curry paste is an obvious partner. You might like
to try adding some finely chopped walnuts when reheating
the purée for added texture and flavour.

Serves 4–6

1 tbsp sunflower oil
1 onion, thinly sliced
1 large garlic clove, crushed
1 tbsp grated fresh root ginger
1 tbsp curry paste
450g/1lb parsnips, thinly sliced
225g/8oz potatoes, peeled and thinly sliced
600ml/1 pint Vegetable Stock (see page 4), plus extra if necessary
2 tbsp dried skimmed milk
salt and freshly ground black pepper

To serve:
thick plain yogurt
chopped fresh coriander or mint

1. Put the oil, onion, garlic and ginger into a large saucepan and
cook gently for about 5 minutes, stirring occasionally, until soft but
not brown. Add the curry paste and cook, stirring gently, for about
2 minutes.

2. Add the parsnips, potatoes and stock. Bring to the boil, cover,
reduce the heat and simmer gently for about 20 minutes or until
the parsnips are really soft.

3. Leave to cool slightly, then tip the mixture into a food processor
or blender and purée until smooth.

4. Add the dried milk and purée again.

5. Season to taste and, if necessary, add some extra stock or water until the soup is the required consistency.

6. Reheat, then ladle into warm bowls, topping each one with a spoonful of yogurt and some chopped fresh coriander or mint.

To microwave:
1. Put the oil, onion, garlic, ginger and curry paste into a large casserole. Cook on High for about 3 minutes until soft, stirring once.

2. Add the parsnips, potatoes and the hot stock. Cover and cook on High for about 12 minutes, stirring once or twice, or until the parsnips are very soft.

3. As steps 3–6.

To slow-cook:
1. Put everything in the slow-cooker, covering in the hot stock.

2. Cover and cook on High for 2 hours or Low for 4–6 hours.

3. Continue as step 3. Serve immediately or tip back in the crockpot and leave on Low until ready to serve.

To freeze:
Cool and freeze at the end of step 5.

COOKS' TIP: Milk powder
Instead of milk or cream, add a spoonful or two of dried skimmed milk powder to a soup. It adds creaminess without the extra liquid and fat.

Cream of Celery and Bacon

Celery is in season from the autumn right through winter into early spring. It is often used as an added flavour in other dishes but makes a wonderful soup in its own right, especially when combined with good-quality bacon from outdoor-reared pigs. Try it braised as a vegetable, too.

Serves 4

40g/1½oz butter
1 onion, finely chopped
1 large garlic clove, crushed
1 celery head, trimmed, separated and thickly sliced
225g/8oz lean back bacon rashers
900ml/1½ pints Chicken Stock (see page 8) or Vegetable Stock (see page 4)
1 tbsp fresh thyme leaves or 1 tsp dried
salt and freshly ground black pepper
3 tbsp dried skimmed milk
1 tsp sunflower oil

1. Melt the butter in a large saucepan and add the onion, garlic and celery. Cook gently for about 15 minutes, stirring occasionally, until the vegetables are soft but not brown.

2. Reserve 4 bacon rashers and finely chop the remainder. Add the chopped bacon to the pan and cook for 2 minutes, stirring occasionally.

3. Add the stock and thyme. Bring to the boil, cover, reduce the heat and simmer gently for about 15 minutes or until the celery is very soft.

4. Leave to cool slightly, then tip the mixture into a food processor or blender and purée until smooth. Season with salt and pepper to taste, add the dried milk and purée again.

5. Cut the remaining bacon into thin strips. Heat the oil in a small non-stick pan and cook the bacon, stirring frequently, until crisp and brown.

6. Reheat the soup gently and serve topped with the crisp bacon pieces.

To microwave:
1. Put the butter, onion, garlic and celery into a large casserole. Cover and cook on High for about 10 minutes, stirring occasionally, until the vegetables are soft.

2. Reserve 4 bacon rashers and finely chop the remainder. Stir the chopped bacon into the casserole, cover and cook on High for 3 minutes, stirring once.

3. Add half the hot stock and the thyme. Cover and cook on High for about 10 minutes or until the celery is very soft, stirring once or twice.

4. Add the remaining stock, then continue as step 4.

5. As steps 5 and 6.

To slow-cook:
1. Reserve 4 bacon rashers and finely chop the remainder. Fry the onion, garlic, celery and the 4 chopped bacon rashers in butter for 2 minutes. Tip into the slow-cooker.

2. Add the hot stock and thyme. Cover and cook on High for 2–3 hours or Low for 5–7 hours.

3. As steps 4–6.

To freeze:
Cool and freeze at the end of step 4. To serve, thaw, then continue as steps 5 and 6.

Carrot and Leek Soup with a Hint of Orange

This light winter vegetable soup is good served as a starter, before a meat dish. Top it with some dainty croûtons and a few thinly pared strips of orange peel (pour boiling water over the strips of peel and leave them to stand while you make the soup).

Serves 4–6

25g/1oz butter
1 onion, finely chopped
3 small leeks, thinly sliced
3 carrots, thinly sliced
1 small potato, peeled and diced
600ml/1 pint Chicken Stock (see page 8) or Vegetable Stock (see page 4)
2 tsp ground coriander
1 orange
about 300ml/½ pint milk
salt and freshly ground black pepper

1. Melt the butter in a large saucepan and add the onion, leeks, carrots and potato. Cook gently for about 10 minutes, stirring occasionally, until soft but not brown.

2. Add the stock and coriander. Finely grate 2 teaspoons of zest from the orange and add to the pot. (Pare a few strips of peel, too, if using for garnish.) Squeeze the juice from the orange and add it too.

3. Bring to the boil, cover and reduce the heat. Simmer gently for about 10 minutes or until the vegetables are very soft.

4. Leave to cool slightly, then tip into a food processor or blender and purée until smooth. Pour in the milk and purée again, adding a little extra if necessary to produce the required consistency. Season with salt and pepper to taste.

5. Reheat and serve.

To microwave:
1. Put the butter, onion, leeks, carrots and potato into a large casserole. Cook on High for about 5 minutes, stirring once or twice, until soft.

2. Add the hot stock and the coriander. Finely grate 2 teaspoons of zest from the orange and add to the casserole. Squeeze the juice from the orange and add it too.

3. Cover and cook on High for about 10 minutes or until the vegetables are very soft, stirring once or twice.

4. As steps 4 and 5.

To slow-cook:
1. Prepare as step 1 and tip into the crockpot.

2. Add the hot stock and remaining ingredients as in step 2.

3. Cover and cook on High for 1–2 hours or Low for 4–6 hours.

4. Continue as step 4. Serve straight away or tip back in the crockpot and leave on Low until ready to serve.

To freeze:
Cool and freeze at the end of step 4.

Sweet Potato and Leek Soup

Sweet potatoes are traditionally grown in warmer climates but do surprisingly well in more temperate areas if protected from the cold by black sacks or in a polytunnel. They make a welcome change from more common tubers and can be treated in exactly the same way. They go particularly well with leeks in this delicious winter warmer.

Serves 4–6

25g/1oz butter
1 tbsp sunflower oil
1 onion, finely chopped
550g/1¼lb leeks, thinly sliced
550g/1¼lb sweet potatoes, cut into 1cm/½in cubes
1 litre/1¾ pints Chicken Stock (see page 8) or Vegetable Stock (see page 4), plus
extra if necessary
salt and freshly ground black pepper
chopped parsley and/or snipped fresh chives, to serve

1. Heat the butter and oil in a large saucepan and add the onion and leeks. Cook gently for about 10 minutes, stirring occasionally, until soft but not brown.

2. Stir in the sweet potatoes and cook for about 5 minutes, stirring occasionally.

3. Add the stock. Bring to the boil, reduce the heat and simmer gently for about 20 minutes until the vegetables are very soft.

4. Leave to cool slightly, then tip into a food processor or blender and purée until smooth (add a little extra stock, if necessary, to make a thick pouring consistency).

5. Season to taste, reheat and serve sprinkled with parsley and/or chives.

To microwave:

1. Put the butter, oil, onion and leeks into a large casserole. Cover and cook on High for 5 minutes, stirring once, until soft.

2. Stir in the sweet potatoes and cook on High for 5 minutes, stirring once.

3. Add half the hot stock. Cook on High for 10–15 minutes or until the vegetables are very soft, stirring once or twice.

4. Add the remaining stock and continue as steps 4 and 5.

To slow-cook:

1. Prepare as step 1 and tip into the crockpot.

2. Add the sweet potatoes and hot stock.

3. Cover and cook on High for 2 hours or Low for 4–6 hours.

4. Continue as step 4. Tip back in the crockpot and leave on Low until ready to serve, garnished with parsley and/or chives.

To freeze:

Cool and freeze at the end of step 4.

COOKS' TIP: Stop potatoes browning

When peeled, some varieties of sweet potato quickly turn black, so prepare them just before they are needed. Alternatively, immerse the pieces in acidulated water (add some lemon juice or vinegar) until required.

Creamy Potato Soup with Nutmeg

Potatoes are available all year round. Maincrop varieties are lifted in the autumn so this recipe could, arguably, go in that section but it is a wonderful soup to serve throughout the winter when you want something simple, warming and soothing so we've included it here. Nutmeg complements potatoes to give a wonderful flavour. Use freshly grated nutmeg if you can.

Serves 4–6

25g/1oz butter
1 onion, thinly sliced
1 large garlic clove, finely chopped
550g/1¼lb potatoes, peeled and sliced
750ml/1¼ pints light Vegetable Stock (see page 4)
salt and freshly ground black pepper
300ml/½ pint milk
¼ tsp grated nutmeg
3 tbsp double cream
chopped fresh parsley, to garnish

1. Melt the butter in a large saucepan and add the onion, garlic and potatoes. Cook gently for about 10 minutes, stirring occasionally, without browning.

2. Add the stock and seasoning. Bring to the boil, cover, reduce the heat and simmer gently for about 25 minutes until the vegetables are very soft.

3. Leave to cool slightly, then tip into a food processor or blender and purée until smooth.

4. Return the soup to the pan and stir in the milk and nutmeg. Bring to the boil, then simmer gently for 5 minutes.

5. Stir in the cream and serve sprinkled with parsley.

To microwave:
1. Put the butter, onion, garlic and potatoes into a large casserole. Cover and cook on High for 5 minutes, stirring once.

2. Add half the hot stock and seasoning. Cover and cook on High for about 15 minutes, stirring once or twice, until the vegetables are very soft.

3. Add the remaining stock then continue as step 3.

4. Return the soup to the casserole and stir in the milk and nutmeg. Cook on High for 5 minutes, stirring once.

5. Continue as step 5.

Not suitable for slow-cooking.

To freeze:
Cool and freeze after adding the milk and nutmeg in step 4. Thaw and reheat the soup, then continue with step 5.

Butterbean Soup with Chorizo

Although neither butter beans nor chorizo are seasonal, this soup
is also flavoured with winter mainstays like celery, potatoes
and carrots. Chorizo has a wonderful smoked paprika flavour
but you could also use smoked pork sausage or even diced,
smoked pancetta instead.

Serves 4–6

25g/1oz butter
1 onion, finely chopped
1 large garlic clove, crushed
1 carrot, thinly sliced
1 celery stick, thinly sliced
1 potato, peeled and sliced
425g/15oz can butter beans
1 litre/1¼ pints Chicken Stock (see page 8) or Vegetable Stock (see page 4)
salt and freshly ground black pepper
1 tbsp olive oil
about 115g/4oz chorizo sausage, thinly sliced

1. Melt the butter in a large saucepan and add the onion. Cook over
a low heat for about 5 minutes, stirring occasionally, or until the
onion is soft and golden brown.

2. Stir in the garlic, carrot, celery and potato. Add the butter beans
(including their juice), stock and seasoning. Bring to the boil, cover,
reduce the heat and simmer gently for about 15 minutes or until
the vegetables are very soft.

3. Leave to cool slightly, then tip into a food processor or blender
and purée until smooth. Return to the pan and season with salt and
pepper to taste.

4. In a small frying pan, heat the oil and quickly cook the sausage, stirring until golden brown. Lift out and drain on kitchen paper.

5. Reheat the soup and serve with the sausage scattered over the top.

To microwave:
1. Put the butter and onion into a casserole. Cover and cook on High for about 3 minutes or until soft, stirring once.

2. Stir in the garlic, carrot, celery and potato. Add the butter beans (including their juice), half the hot stock and the seasoning. Cover and cook on High for about 10 minutes, stirring once or twice, or until the vegetables are very soft.

3. Add the remaining stock and continue as step 3.

4. As steps 4 and 5.

To slow-cook:
1. Prepare as step 1 and tip into the crockpot.

2. Add the garlic, carrot, celery, potato. butter beans and their juice, hot stock and seasoning.

3. Cover and cook on High for 2 hours or Low for 4–6 hours.

4. Continue as step 3 to 5. If not serving immediately, tip the soup back in the crockpot and leave on Low until ready to serve, garnished with the chorizo scattered over.

To freeze:
Cool and freeze at the end of step 3. Thaw, then continue as steps 4 and 5.

Mulligatawny Soup

This Anglo-Indian dish is a popular favourite in British households. It's the perfect soup to warm you up on a winter's day, made with good, basic winter vegetables. Use mild, medium or hot curry powder, according to your taste. Naan bread is the ideal accompaniment here.

Serves 4–6

40g/1½oz butter

1 large onion, thinly sliced

1 small carrot, finely chopped

2 small celery sticks, thinly sliced

¼ small swede, finely chopped

1 large garlic clove, finely chopped

25g/1oz plain flour

2 tsp curry powder or paste

1.2 litres/2 pints Chicken Stock (see page 8)

1 large cooking apple

2 tsp lemon juice

25g/1oz basmati rice

25–55g/1–2oz cooked chicken meat, cut into shreds

salt and freshly ground black pepper

4 tbsp single cream

2 tbsp chopped fresh coriander leaves

1. Melt the butter in a large saucepan and stir in the onion, carrot, celery, swede and garlic. Cook gently for about 10 minutes, stirring occasionally, until soft but not brown.

2. Stir in the flour and curry powder or paste and cook, stirring, for 2–3 minutes. Gradually blend in the stock and cook, stirring, until the mixture comes to the boil and thickens slightly. Cover, reduce the heat and simmer gently for 30 minutes, stirring occasionally.

3. Peel, core and dice the apple and add to the pan with the lemon juice, rice and chicken. Season with salt and pepper.

4. Cover and simmer gently for about 15 minutes, or until the rice is tender.

5. Stir in the cream and coriander and serve.

To microwave:
1. Put the butter, onion, carrot, celery, swede and garlic into a large casserole. Cover and cook on High for about 5 minutes, stirring once or twice, until soft.

2. Stir in the flour and curry powder or paste and cook, uncovered, for 2 minutes. Gradually blend in half the hot stock. Cook on High for about 5 minutes, stirring once or twice, until the mixture comes to the boil and thickens. Cover and cook on Medium for 10 minutes, stirring once.

3. As step 3.

4. Add the remaining hot stock. Cover and cook on High for about 10 minutes or until the rice is tender.

5. As step 5.

To slow-cook:
1. Prepare as steps 1 and 2 and tip into the crockpot.

2. Cover and cook on High for 2–3 hours or Low for 4–6 hours.

3. Continue as step 3 and cook on High for a further 1 hour or Low for a further 2 hours.

4. As step 5.

Not suitable for freezing.

Lentil and Bacon Soup

Serve this with a generous hunk of crusty bread. I like to top the soup with a swirl of double cream or some grated cheese.

Serves 6

1 tbsp oil
115g/4oz lean streaky bacon, rinds removed and chopped
1 large onion, finely chopped
2 carrots, chopped,
¼ celeriac, chopped
225g/8oz red lentils
1.5 litres/2¾ pints ham, Chicken Stock (see page 8)
or Vegetable Stock (see page 4)
2 tbsp tomato purée
salt and freshly ground black pepper

1. Heat the oil in a large saucepan and cook the bacon, stirring occasionally until it just begins to brown.

2. Stir in the onion, carrots and celeriac and cook gently for about 5 minutes, stirring occasionally, until the onions are pale golden brown.

3. Stir in the lentils, stock and the tomato purée. Bring to the boil, cover, reduce the heat and simmer gently for about 30 minutes until the lentils and vegetables are very soft.

4. Leave to cool slightly, then tip into a food processor or blender and purée until smooth.

5. Season with salt and pepper to taste, reheat and serve.

To microwave:

1. Put the oil and bacon into a large casserole. Cook on High for 3 minutes, stirring once.

2. Add the onion, carrots and celeriac. Cover and cook on High for about 5 minutes, stirring once, until the onions are very soft.

3. Stir in the lentils, half the hot stock and the tomato purée. Cook on High for about 5 minutes or until the mixture comes to the boil, stirring once, then cover and cook on Medium-Low for about 30 minutes until the lentils and vegetables are very soft, stirring once or twice. Add the remaining stock, then continue as step 4.

4. As step 5.

To slow-cook:

1. Prepare as steps 1 and 2 and tip into the crockpot.

2. Add the lentils, hot stock and tomato purée.

3. Cover and cook on High for 2–3 hours or Low for 5–7 hours.

4. Continue as step 4 and either serve straight away or return to the crockpot and leave on Low until ready to serve.

To freeze:

Cool and freeze at the end of step 4.

Scotch Broth with Lamb

A quick, modern version of a traditional winter-warming dish that celebrates the best of British produce. The pearl barley and dried peas enrich and thicken the soup. For a more economical version, use a meaty lamb bone left over from the Sunday roast. Put it in the pot and start at step 2. Lift the bone out at the end of step 4, cut all the meat off it, cut the meat into neat pieces, if necessary, and return to the pot before stirring in the parsley.

Serves 6

1 tbsp oil
6 lean best-end-of-neck lamb cutlets, trimmed of excess fat
1.5 litres/2¾ pints lamb stock (see page 6)
3 tbsp pearl barley
4 tbsp dried green peas, soaked in cold water overnight and drained
1 large onion, finely chopped
1 large carrot, diced
½ small swede, diced
salt and freshly ground black pepper
about 175g/6oz cabbage, shredded
2 leeks, thinly sliced
4 tbsp chopped fresh parsley

1. Heat the oil in a large saucepan and quickly brown the lamb on all sides.

2. Add the stock, barley and peas. Bring to the boil, cover and simmer gently for 30 minutes.

3. Add the onion, carrot, swede and seasoning. Bring to the boil and cover. Reduce the heat and simmer gently for a further 30 minutes or until the barley and vegetables are soft.

4. Stir in the cabbage and leeks. Bring to the boil, then cover and simmer gently for a final 10–15 minutes.

5. Stir in the parsley. Serve each person with a lamb chop, some vegetables and plenty of the broth.

To microwave:

1. As step 1.

2. Transfer the lamb to a large casserole and add half the hot stock, the barley and peas. Cook on High for about 5 minutes or until just boiling, stirring once. Cover and cook on Medium for 20 minutes, stirring once or twice.

3. Add the onion, carrot, swede and seasoning. Cook on High for about 5 minutes or until the mixture comes to the boil. Cover and cook on Medium for 30 minutes, or until the barley and vegetables are soft, stirring once or twice.

4. Stir in the cabbage and leeks. Cook on High for about 5 minutes or until boiling, stirring once. Cover and cook on Medium for 10 minutes.

5. As step 5.

To slow-cook:

1. Prepare as step 1 and tip into the crockpot.

2. Add the hot stock and remaining ingredients, apart from the parsley.

3. Cover and cook on High for 2–3 hours or Low for 5–7 hours.

4. Continue as step 5.

Not suitable for freezing.

Chilli Beef and Red Bean Soup

A robust soup which needs only some good fresh bread to
accompany it. Adjust the amount of chilli sauce to suit
your own taste.

Serves 4

1 tbsp oil
1 large onion, finely chopped
1 large garlic clove, finely chopped
1 parsnip, diced
1 carrot, diced
1 tsp caster sugar
225g/8oz frying steak, cut into thin strips
400g/14oz can chopped tomatoes
750ml/1¼ pints beef stock (see Cooks' tip)
2 tbsp chopped fresh herbs or 1 tsp dried mixed herbs
about 1 tsp hot chilli sauce
400g/14oz can red kidney beans, drained
salt and freshly ground black pepper

1. Heat the oil in a large saucepan and add the onion, garlic,
parsnip, carrot and sugar. Cook gently for about 10 minutes,
stirring occasionally, until soft and golden brown.

2. Stir in the steak and cook for about 5 minutes, stirring occasionally, until brown.

3. Add the tomatoes, stock, herbs, chilli sauce and beans. Bring
to the boil, cover, reduce the heat and simmer gently for about
20 minutes, or until the steak is tender.

4. Season with salt and pepper to taste.

To microwave:
1. Put the oil, onion, garlic, parsnip, carrot and sugar into a large casserole. Cover and cook on High for about 5 minutes, stirring once, or until soft.

2. Stir in the steak and cook for 3 minutes, stirring once.

3. Add the tomatoes, hot stock, herbs, chilli sauce and beans. Cover and cook on High for about 10 minutes, or until the mixture comes to the boil. Stir, cover and cook on Medium for about 20 minutes or until the steak is tender, stirring once or twice.

4. Season with salt and pepper to taste.

To slow-cook:
1. Prepare as steps 1 and 2 and tip into the crockpot.

2. Add the tomatoes, hot stock and remaining ingredients.

3. Cover and cook on High for 2–3 hours or Low for 5–7 hours. Taste and re-season.

Not suitable for freezing.

COOKS' TIP: Consommé
In place of beef stock, you could use a can of good-quality consommé, made up to 700ml/1¼ pints with water.

Celery and Stilton Soup

The traditional partnership of celery with Stilton, both best in winter, makes a filling soup with a rich flavour. If you prefer, purée all the soup. You may then need to rub it through a sieve, too, to remove any strings from the celery. Serve with plenty of fresh crusty bread.

Serves 6

40g/1½oz butter
1 onion, finely chopped
1 potato, peeled and chopped
1 head of celery, thinly sliced, reserving the leaves for garnish
900ml/1½ pints Chicken Stock (see page 8) or Vegetable Stock (see page 4)
salt and freshly ground black pepper
85g/3oz Stilton cheese
150ml/¼ pint single cream

1. Melt the butter in a large saucepan and cook the onion gently for about 5 minutes, stirring occasionally, until soft but not brown.

2. Stir in the potato and celery. Cook over medium heat for 5 minutes, stirring occasionally, without browning.

3. Add the stock and season with pepper. Bring to the boil, cover, reduce the heat and simmer gently for about 30 minutes or until the vegetables are very soft.

4. Leave to cool slightly then tip three-quarters of the mixture into a food processor or blender. Purée until smooth.

5. Return the purée to the pan and stir well. Reheat and adjust the seasoning if necessary.

6. Remove from the heat, crumble in half the cheese and stir in the cream. Once the cheese has melted into the soup, serve, crumbling a little of the remaining cheese on top of each bowl and garnish with reserved celery leaves.

To microwave:

1. Put the butter and onion into a large casserole and cook on High for about 3 minutes, stirring once, until soft.

2. Stir in the potato and celery. Cover and cook on High for 5 minutes, stirring once.

3. Add half the hot stock and season with pepper. Cover and cook on High for about 15 minutes or until the vegetables are very soft, stirring once or twice.

4. Add the remaining stock and continue as step 4.

5. As steps 5 and 6.

To slow-cook:

1. Prepare as step 1 and tip into the crockpot.

2. Add the hot stock and remaining ingredients.

3. Cover and cook on High for 2–3 hours or Low for 5–7 hours.

4. As step 5.

To freeze:

Cool and freeze at the end of step 5. Thaw, reheat and complete as step 6.

Vegetable Soup with Cheddar and Mustard

Ideal for serving on a chilly day, this recipe, again, makes the most of the robust winter vegetables. Here they're spiked with Dijon mustard and well-flavoured Cheddar cheese to enrich and add more nourishing goodness. For a change from bread, try serving it with oatcakes or some freshly-baked herb scones.

Serves 4

25g/1oz butter
1 onion, finely chopped
1 leek, thinly sliced
4 carrots, thinly sliced
2 celery sticks, thinly sliced
450ml/¾ pint Vegetable Stock (see page 4)
300ml/½ pint milk
25g/1oz plain flour
1 tbsp Dijon or wholegrain mustard
115g/4oz mature Cheddar cheese, grated
salt and freshly ground black pepper

1. Melt the butter in a large saucepan. Add the vegetables and fry gently, stirring, for 3 minutes to soften slightly. Add the stock, bring to the boil and cover. Reduce the heat and simmer gently for about 25 minutes, or until the vegetables are very tender.

2. Gradually blend the milk into the flour until smooth, then stir into the pan. Cook, stirring, until the soup comes to the boil.

3. Reduce the heat again and simmer gently for 5 minutes. Stir in the mustard.

4. Remove the pan from the heat and add half the cheese. Stir until it has melted. Season to taste.

5. Ladle into warm bowls and serve sprinkled with the remaining cheese.

To microwave:
1. Put the butter and vegetables into a large casserole and cook on High for 5 minutes, stirring once. Add half the hot stock. Cover and cook on High for about 10 minutes, stirring occasionally, or until the vegetables are very tender.

2. Gradually blend the milk into the flour, then stir into the casserole. Cook on High for about 5 minutes, stirring occasionally, or until the soup comes to the boil.

3. Cover and cook on Medium for 5 minutes. Stir in the mustard.

4. Add the remaining hot stock, then continue as steps 4 and 5.

To slow-cook:
1. Prepare as step 1 and tip into the crockpot.

2. Add the hot stock and remaining ingredients.

3. Cover and cook on High for 2–3 hours or Low for 5–7 hours.

4. As step 5.

Not suitable for freezing.

Jerusalem Artichoke Soup

Jerusalem artichokes make a fabulous roast winter vegetable (they're particularly good with game birds) but they also make the most wonderful velvety soup. Choose ones with the least knobbly bits as they're easier to peel or scrub.

Serves 4

675g/1½lb Jerusalem artichokes
1 tbsp lemon juice
2 tbsp sunflower oil
1 large onion, chopped
1 large potato, peeled and diced
900ml/1½ pints Chicken Stock (see page 8) or Vegetable Stock (see page 4)
1 bay leaf
salt and freshly ground black pepper
120ml/4fl oz crème fraîche
a little freshly grated nutmeg
chopped parsley, to serve

1. Peel or scrub the artichokes, cut into chunks and place in water with the lemon juice added until ready to cook. Heat the oil in a large saucepan, add the onion and fry very gently, stirring, for 3 minutes until softened but not browned.

2. Add the drained artichokes, the potato, stock, bay leaf and a little salt and pepper. Bring to the boil, reduce the heat, partially cover and simmer gently for about 20 minutes until the vegetables are really soft.

3. Discard the bay leaf and purée in a blender or food processor until really smooth. Return to the large saucepan and stir in 100ml/3½fl oz) of the crème fraîche. Reheat, taste and re-season if necessary. Add a little grated nutmeg to taste.

4. Serve hot in warm soup bowls with a spoonful of the remaining crème fraîche in each and a sprinkling of chopped parsley.

To microwave:

1. As step 1 but put the oil and onion in a large casserole and cook on High for 2 minutes, stirring once.

2. Continue as step 2 but add hot stock. Microwave on High for about 12 minutes, stirring once or twice until the artichokes are tender.

3. Continue as step 3 but return to the microwave to reheat on High for 1–2 minutes. Continue as step 4.

To slow-cook:

1. As step 1. Tip into the slow-cooker.

2. Continue as step 2 but add hot stock. Cover and cook on High for 3–4 hours or Low for 6–8 hours.

3. Continue as step 3. Tip back in the slow-cooker and leave on Low for at least 5 minutes to heat through.

4. Continue as step 4.

To freeze:

Cool, then freeze before adding the crème fraîche. To serve, thaw completely then reheat thoroughly, stir in the crème fraîche and continue as steps 3 and 4.

Chestnut and Celeriac Velouté

Some of us may remember roasting chestnuts over the open fire at home in our youth (or buying them from the chestnut seller with his brazier on a chilly street corner). The downside is they are a fiddle to prepare but the flavour is fantastic. You can cheat with a 240g/8oz can of ready-prepared ones.

Serves 4

400g/14oz chestnuts in their shells
25g/1oz butter
2 tbsp sunflower oil
1 large onion, chopped
½ celeriac, peeled and diced
1 large potato, peeled and diced
2 large sprigs of thyme
750ml/1¼ pints Chicken Stock (see page 8) or Vegetable Stock (see page 4)
salt and freshly ground black pepper
1 egg yolk
6 tbsp double cream

1. First prepare the chestnuts. Make a slit in each shell on the flat side. Place in a saucepan, cover with cold water, bring to the boil, drain and leave to cool. Carefully peel off the hard outer shell and the brown inner skin.

2. Melt the butter in a saucepan with the oil, add the onion and fry gently, stirring for 2–3 minutes until softened but not browned. Add the chestnuts, celeriac, potato, thyme, stock and salt and pepper. Bring to the boil, reduce the heat and simmer gently for 20–30 minutes until the nuts and celeriac are really tender.

3. Discard the thyme then purée the mixture in a blender or food processor. If necessary, rub through a sieve to ensure the mixture is completely smooth.

4. Return the mixture to the saucepan and season to taste with salt and pepper. Whisk 4 tbsp of the cream with the egg yolk until smooth (reserve the remainder for garnish). Stir into the soup. Reheat but on no account allow to boil or the mixture will curdle. Ladle into warm open soup plates and add a swirl of the remaining cream to each.

To microwave:
1. Make a slit in the flat side of each chestnut. Put six at a time in a bowl. Cover with clingfilm, rolled back slightly at one edge and microwave for 30 seconds until the skins split. Tip out then peel.

2. Repeat until all the chestnuts are peeled.

3. Melt the butter and oil in a casserole. Add the onion, cover and cook on High for 2 minutes, stirring once.

4. Add the remaining ingredients except the egg yolk and cream. Cover and cook on High for 20 minutes, stirring occasionally, until everything is tender.

5. Continue as step 3.

6. Return to the casserole and continue as step 4. After stirring in the cream and egg yolk, Cook on Medium-Low for a minute or two to heat through, stirring once, but do not allow to boil. Stir and serve as step 4.

To slow-cook:
1. As steps 1 and 2 but tip the fried onions into the slow-cooker. Add the chestnuts, celeriac, potato, thyme, hot stock and seasoning. Cover and cook on High for 2 hours or Low for 4–6 hours until everything is tender.

2. Continue as steps 3 and 4 but return to the slow-cooker. Cover and leave on Low for 2 minutes to heat through before stirring and serving.

Index